THE MOM TEST

HOW TO TALK TO CUSTOMERS AND LEARN IF YOUR BUSINESS IS A GOOD IDEA WHEN EVERYONE IS LYING TO YOU

ROB FITZPATRICK

CONTENTS

Introduction v

1. The Mom Test 1
2. Avoiding bad data 17
3. Asking important questions 39
4. Keeping it casual 57
5. Commitment and advancement 65
6. Finding conversations 77
7. Choosing your customers 95
8. Running the process 105

Conclusion and cheatsheet 119
Acknowledgments 127

INTRODUCTION

Trying to learn from customer conversations is like excavating a delicate archaeological site. The truth is down there somewhere, but it's fragile. While each blow with your shovel gets you closer to the truth, you're liable to smash it into a million little pieces if you use too blunt an instrument.

I see a lot of teams using a bulldozer and crate of dynamite for their excavation. They are, in one way or another, forcing people to say something nice about their business. They use heavy-handed questions like "do you think it's a good idea" and shatter their prize.

At the other end of the spectrum, some founders are using a toothbrush to unearth a city, flinching away from digging deep and finding out whether anything of value is actually buried down there.

We want to find the truth of how to make our business succeed. We need to dig for it—and dig deep—but every question we ask carries the very real possibility of biasing the person we're talking to and rendering the whole exercise pointless. It happens more than you'd ever imagine.

The truth is our goal and questions are our tools. But we must learn to wield them. It's delicate work. And well worth learning. There's treasure below.

TALKING TO CUSTOMERS IS HARD

We know we *ought* to talk to customers. Many of us even *do* talk to customers. But we still end up building stuff nobody buys. Isn't that exactly what talking to people is meant to prevent?

It turns out almost all of us are doing it wrong. I've made these mistakes myself and seen them happen a hundred times over with other founders. Despite the recent explosion of startup knowledge, the process of figuring out what customers want too often unfolds as it did at my first company, Habit.

We were building social advertising tech and I was distraught. We'd spent 3 years working our hearts out. We'd nearly run out of investor money and it didn't look like we'd be getting more. We'd relocated internationally to be closer to our market and had survived a co-founder being deported. I'd been talking to customers full-time for months. And then, after innumerable days of slog and an exhausted team, I learned I'd been doing it wrong. I may as well not have bothered.

The advice that you "should talk to customers" is well-intentioned, but ultimately a bit unhelpful. It's like the popular kid advising his nerdy friend to "just be cooler." You still have to know how to actually do it.

These conversations take time, are easy to screw up and go wrong in a nefarious way. Bad customer conversations aren't just useless. Worse, they convince you that you're on the right path. They give you a false positive that causes you to over-invest your cash, your time, and your team. Even when you're not actively screwing something up, those pesky customers seem hellbent on lying to you.

This book is a practical how-to. The approach and tools within are gathered from a wide range of communities including Customer Development, Design Thinking, Lean Startup, User Experience, traditional sales and more. It's based on working with a bunch of founders and from my experiences both failing and succeeding at customer learning, as well as from the support of innumerable peers and mentors.

It's a casual approach to conversation, based on chipping away the formality and awkwardness of talking to people and taking full responsibility for asking good questions.

WHY ANOTHER BOOK ON TALKING AND SELLING?

Does your shelf really need another book on selling and talking? And does it need one written by me in particular?

Well... yes. Yes it does.

Here's why:

Firstly, I'm a techie, not a sales guy. I'm introverted and naturally bad in meetings. Every other sales book I've read is written by and for folks who are already pretty good at dealing with people. They know the unspoken rules of the meeting. I fumbled through from scratch. You know that line, "Don't call me, I'll call you"? People have actually said that to me (and I believed them). With much help from peers and advisors, I eventually started figuring it out and we closed deals with companies like Sony and MTV. But I learned that there's a big gap between textbooks and check books.

Secondly, before we can start doing things correctly, we need to understand how we're doing them wrong. Through my own projects and my work with new founders, I've built up an exhaustive list of how it can go wrong. Throughout the book, I'll try to help you see where you might be messing stuff up in unnoticed ways.

Finally, this is a practical handbook, not a theoretical tome. For example, how do you find people to talk to and set up the meetings? How do you take notes while still being polite and paying attention? It's all in here.

I can't teach you how to make your business huge. That's up to you. But I *can* give you the tools to talk to customers, navigate the noise, and learn what they really want. The saddest thing that can happen to a startup is for nobody to care when it disappears. We're going to make sure that doesn't happen.

A NOTE ON SCOPE & TERMINOLOGY

This book isn't a summary or description or re-interpretation of the process of Customer Development. That's a bigger concept and something Steve Blank has covered comprehensively in *4 Steps to the Epiphany* and *The Startup Owner's Manual*.

This book is specifically about how to properly talk to customers and learn from them. Talking is one of the big aspects of Customer Development, but shouldn't be confused with the whole process. To keep the distinction clear, I'm going to refer to chatting with people as "customer conversation" (lowercase) instead of "Customer Development" (uppercase).

For the most part, I'm assuming you already agree that talking to customers is a good idea. I'm not trying to convince you again, so this book is more "how" than "why".

Let's get involved.

CHAPTER 1

THE MOM TEST

People say you shouldn't ask your mom whether your business is a good idea. That's technically true, but it misses the point. You shouldn't ask *anyone* whether your business is a good idea. At least not in those words. Your mom will lie to you the most (just 'cuz she loves you), but it's a bad question and invites everyone to lie to you at least a little.

It's not anyone else's responsibility to show us the truth. It's our responsibility to find it. We do that by asking good questions.

The Mom Test is a set of simple rules for crafting good questions that even your mom can't lie to you about.

Before we get there, let's look at two conversations with mom and see what we can learn about our business idea: digital cookbooks for the iPad.

FAILING THE MOM TEST

Son: "Mom, mom, I have an idea for a business — can I

run it by you?" *I am about to expose my ego — please don't hurt my feelings.*

Mom: "Of course, dear." *You are my only son and I am ready to lie to protect you.*

Son: "You like your iPad, right? You use it a lot?"
Mom: "Yes." *You led me to this answer, so here you go.*

Son: "Okay, so would you ever buy an app which was like a cookbook for your iPad?" *I am optimistically asking a hypothetical question and you know what I want you to say.*

Mom: "Hmmm." *As if I need another cookbook at my age.*

Son: "And it only costs $40 — that's cheaper than those hardcovers on your shelf." *I'm going to skip that lukewarm signal and tell you more about my great idea.*

Mom: "Well..." *Aren't apps supposed to cost a dollar?*

Son: "And you can share recipes with your friends, and there's an iPhone app which is your shopping list. And videos of that celebrity chef you love." *Please just say "yes." I will not leave you alone until you do.*

Mom: "Oh, well yes honey, that sounds amazing. And you're right, $40 *is* a good deal. Will it have pictures of the recipes?" *I have rationalised the price outside of a real purchase decision, made a non-committal compliment, and offered a feature request to appear engaged.*

Son: "Yes, definitely. Thanks mom — love you!" *I have completely mis-interpreted this conversation and taken it as validation.*

Mom: "Won't you have some lasagna?" *I am concerned that you won't be able to afford food soon. Please eat something.*

Our misguided entrepreneur has a few more conversations like this, becomes increasingly convinced he's right, quits his job, and sinks his savings into the app. Then he wonders why nobody (even his mom) buys it, especially since he had been so *rigorous*.

Doing it wrong is worse than doing nothing at all. When you know you're clueless, you tend to be careful. But collecting a fistful of false positives is like convincing a drunk he's sober: not an improvement.

Let's fix the conversation and show that if we do it right, even mom can help us figure out whether our business is a good idea.

PASSING THE MOM TEST

Son: "Hey mom, how's that new iPad treating you?"

Mom: "Oh - I love it! I use it every day."

Son: "What do you usually do on it?" *Whoops — we asked a generic question, so answer to this probably won't be terribly valuable.*

Mom: "Oh, you know. Read the news, play sudoku, catch up with my friends. The usual."

Son: "What's the last thing you did on it?" *Get specific about examples in the past to get real, concrete data.*

Mom: "You know your father and I are planning that trip? I was figuring out where we could stay." *She uses it for both entertainment and utility, which didn't come up during the "usually" answer.*

Son: "Did you use an app for that?" *A slightly leading question, but sometimes we need to nudge to get to the topic we're interested in.*

Mom: "No, I just used Google. I didn't know there was an app. What's it called?" *Younger folks use the App Store as a search engine, whereas your mom waits for a specific recommendation. If that's true more broadly, finding a reliable marketing channel outside the App Store is going to be crucial.*

Son: "How did you find out about the other apps you have?" *Dig into interesting and unexpected answers to understand the behaviours and motivations behind them.*

Mom: "The Sunday paper has a section on the apps of the week." *You can't remember the last time you opened a paper, but it sounds like traditional PR might be a viable option for reaching customers like mom.*
Son: "Makes sense. Hey, by the way, I saw a couple new cookbooks on the shelf — where did those come from?" *Business ideas usually have several failure points. Here it's both the medium of an iPad app and the content of a cookbook.*

> Mom: "They're one of those things you just end up getting at Christmas. I think Marcy gave me that one. Haven't even opened it. As if I need another lasagna recipe at my age!" *Aha! This answer is golden for 3 reasons: 1. Old people don't need another generic set of recipes. 2. The gift market may be strong . 3. Younger cooks may be a better customer segment since they don't yet know the basics.*

> Son: "What's the last cookbook you did buy for yourself?" *Attack generic answers like "I don't buy cookbooks" by asking for specific examples.*

> Mom: "Now that you mention it, I bought a vegan cookbook about 3 months ago. Your father is trying to eat healthier and thought my veggies could benefit from a pinch more zazz." *More gold: experienced chefs may still buy specialised or niche cookbooks.*

The conversation continues. If it's going well, I would raise the topics of whether she has ever looked for recipes on the iPad or searched for cooking videos on YouTube.

You thank her for the lasagna, pet the dog, and head home. You've learned that building an app and waiting for people to find it on the App Store probably isn't a good plan. But you've got some good insight about your customer segment and a few promising leads to look into. That was a useful conversation.

A USEFUL CONVERSATION

The measure of usefulness of an early customer conversation is whether it gives us concrete facts about our customers' lives and world views. These facts, in turn, help us improve our business.

Our original idea looked like this: old people like cookbooks and iPads. Therefore, we will build a cookbook for the iPad. It's generic. There are a thousand possible variations of this premise.

With an idea this vague, we can't answer any of the difficult questions like which recipes to include or how people will hear about it. Until we get specific, it always seems like a good idea.

After just one conversation (with our mom, of all people), we have a higher fidelity vision. We now see that there are at least 2 specific customer segments we might serve, each of which needs a slightly different product. We've also identified some major risks to address before we commit too heavily.

1. We could offer niche recipes (ethnic, diets) which experienced cooks may not already know. Our biggest question is how to reach them when they don't search for apps. We have a possible lead with newspaper and magazine PR.
2. Alternately, we might make generic recipes for younger cooks who are easier to reach via the App Store and who haven't memorised all their favourites yet. We haven't talked to any, so we have loads of questions, but one big one might be whether a customer segment who isn't already in the habit of buying expensive cookbooks will pay a premium for ours.

The first conversation gave us rope to hang ourselves. The second gave us actionable insight. Why? What was different about the second conversation?

Mom was unable to lie to us because we never talked about our idea.

That's kind of weird, right? We find out if people care about what we're doing by never mentioning it. Instead, we talk about them and their lives.

The point is a bit more subtle than this. Eventually you do need to mention what you're building and take people's money for it. However, the big mistake is almost always to mention your idea too soon rather than too late.

If you just avoid mentioning your idea, you automatically start asking better questions. Doing this is the easiest (and biggest) improvement you can make to your customer conversations.

Here are 3 simple rules to help you. They are collectively called (drumroll) The Mom Test:

The Mom Test:

1. Talk about their life instead of your idea
2. Ask about specifics in the past instead of generics or opinions about the future
3. Talk less and listen more

It's called The Mom Test because it leads to questions that even your mom can't lie to you about. When you do it right, they won't even know you have an idea. There are some other important tools and tricks that we'll introduce throughout the rest of the book. But first, let's let's put The Mom Test to work on some questions.

Rule of thumb: Customer conversations are bad by default. It's your job to fix them.

GOOD QUESTION / BAD QUESTION

Are the following questions good or bad? Do they pass or fail The Mom Test? If they fail it, why? And how could we improve them? Work your way through the list and then read on for some discussion.

"Do you think it's a good idea?"
"Would you buy a product which did X?"
"How much would you pay for X?"
"What would your dream product do?"
"Why do you bother?"
"What are the implications of that?"
"Talk me through the last time that happened."
"Talk me through your workflow."
"What else have you tried?"
"Would you pay X for a product which did Y?"
"How are you dealing with it now?"
"Where does the money come from?"
"Who else should I talk to?"
"Is there anything else I should have asked?"

"Do you think it's a good idea?"

Awful question! Here's the thing: only the market can tell if your idea is good. Everything else is just opinion. Unless you're talking to a deep industry expert, this is self-indulgent noise with a high risk of false positives.

Let's fix it: Say you're building an app to help construction companies manage their suppliers. You might ask them to show you how they currently do it. Talk about which parts they love and hate. Ask which other tools and processes they tried before settling on this one. Are they actively searching for a replacement? If so, what's the sticking point? If not, why not? Where are they losing money with their current tools? Is there a budget for better ones? Now, take all that information and decide for yourself whether it's a good idea.

Rule of thumb: Opinions are worthless.

"Would you buy a product which did X?"

Bad question. You're asking for opinions and hypotheticals from overly optimistic people who want to make you happy. The answer to a question like this is almost always "yes", which makes it worthless.

Let's fix it: Ask how they currently solve X and how much it costs them to do so. And how much time it takes. Ask them to talk you through what happened the last time X came up. If they haven't solved the problem, ask why not. Have they tried searching for solutions and found them wanting? Or do they not even care enough to have Googled for it?

Rule of thumb: Anything involving the future is an over-optimistic lie.

"How much would you pay for X?"

Bad question. This is exactly as bad as the last one, except it's more likely to trick you because the number makes it feel rigorous and truthy.

How to fix it: Just like the others, fix it by asking about their life *as it already is*. How much does the problem cost them? How much do they currently pay to solve it? How big is the budget they've allocated? I hope you're noticing a trend here.

Rule of thumb: People will lie to you if they think it's what you want to hear.

"What would your dream product do?"

Sort-of-okay question, but only if you ask good follow-ups. Otherwise it's a bad question. A question like this is like the "set" before the spike in a volleyball game: not too helpful on its own, but it puts you in a good position as long as you're ready to exploit it.

Let's improve it: The value comes from understanding why they want these features. You don't want to just collect feature requests. You aren't building the product by committee. But the motivations and constraints behind those requests are critical.

Rule of thumb: People know what their problems are, but they don't know how to solve those problems.

"Why do you bother?"

Good question. I love this sort of question. It's great for getting from the perceived problem to the real one.

For example, some founders I knew were talking to finance guys spending hours each day sending emails about their spreadsheets. The finance guys were asking for better messaging tools so they could save time. The "why do you bother" question led to "so we can be certain that we're all working off the latest version." Aha. The solution ended up being less like the requested messaging tool and more like Dropbox. A question like "why do you bother" points toward their motivations. It gives you the why.

Rule of thumb: You're shooting blind until you understand their goals.

"What are the implications of that?"

Good question. This distinguishes between I-will-pay-to-solve-that problems and thats-kind-of-annoying-but-I-can-deal-with-it "problems". Some problems have big, costly implications. Others exist but don't actually matter. It behooves you to find out which is which. It also gives you a good pricing signal.

I once had someone keep describing the workflow we were fixing with emotionally loaded terms like "DISASTER", accompanied by much yelling and arm waving. But when I asked him what the implications were, he sort of shrugged and said "Oh, we just ended up throwing a bunch of interns at the problem—it's actually working pretty well."

Rule of thumb: Some problems don't actually matter.

"Talk me through the last time that happened."

Good question. Your high school writing teacher may have told you that stories are meant to "show, not tell". Whenever possible, you want to be shown, not told, by your customers. Learn through their actions instead of their opinions. If you ran a burger joint, it would be stupid to survey your customers about whether they prefer cheeseburgers or hamburgers. Just watch what they buy (but if you're trying to understand *why* they prefer one over the other, you'll have to talk to them).

Folks can't be wishy-washy when you're watching them do the task in question. Get as close to the real action as you can. Seeing it first hand provides unique insight into murky situations.

But if you can't get in there, asking them to talk you through the last time it happened is still a huge help.

Being walked through their full workflow answers many questions in one fell swoop: how do they spend their days, what tools do they use, and who do they talk to? What are the constraints of their day and life? How does your product fit into that day? Which other tools, products, software, and tasks does your product need to integrate with?

Rule of thumb: Watching someone do a task will show you where the problems and inefficiencies really are, not where the customer thinks they are.

"What else have you tried?"

Good question. What are they using now? How much does it cost and what do they love or hate about it? How much would those fixes be worth and how traumatic would it be for them to switch to a new solution?

I was checking out an idea with a potential customer and they excitedly said, "Oh man, that happens all the time. I would *definitely* pay for something which solved that problem."

That's a future-promise statement without any commitment to back it up, so I needed to learn whether it was true or not. I asked, "When's the last time this came up?" Turns out, it was pretty recent. That's a great sign. To dig further, I asked, "Can you talk me through how you tried to fix it?" He looked at me blankly, so I nudged him further.

"Did you google around for any other ways to solve it?" He seemed a little bit like he'd been caught stealing from the cookie jar and said, "No... I didn't really think to. It's something I'm used to dealing with, you know?"

In the abstract, it's something he would "definitely" pay to solve. Once we got specific, he didn't even care enough to search for a solution (which do exist, incidentally).

It's easy to get someone emotional about a problem if you lead them there. "Don't you *hate* when your shoelaces come untied while you're carrying groceries?" "Yeah, that's the *worst*!" And then I go off and design my special never-come-untied laces without realising that if you actually cared, you would already be using a double-knot.

Rule of thumb: If they haven't looked for ways of solving it already, they're not going to look for (or buy) yours.

"Would you pay X for a product which did Y?"

Bad question. The fact that you've added a number doesn't help. This is bad for the same reasons as the others: people are overly optimistic about what they *would* do and want to make you happy. Plus, it's about your idea instead of their life.

Let's fix it: As always, ask about what they already do now, not what they believe they might do in the future. Common wisdom is that you price your product in terms of value to the customer rather than cost to you. That's true. And you can't quantify the value received without prodding their financial worldview.

Another way to fix it, if you're far enough along, is to literally ask for money. If you have the deposit or pre-order in hand, you know they're telling the truth.

Rule of thumb: People stop lying when you ask them for money.

"How are you dealing with it now?"

Good question. Beyond workflow information, this gives you a price anchor. If they're paying £100/month for a duct-tape workaround, you know which ballpark you're playing in. On the other hand, they may have spent £120,000 this year on agency fees to maintain a site you're replacing. If that's the case, you don't want to be having the £100 conversation.

Sometimes, both of the above will be happening simultaneously and you get to choose how you present yourself. Do you want to be a replacement for the web app at a yearly value of £1.2k or for the agency at 100x that?

Rule of thumb: While it's rare for someone to tell you precisely what they'll pay you, they'll often show you what it's worth to them.

"Where does the money come from?"

Good question. This isn't something you would necessarily ask a consumer (though you might), but in a B2B context it's a must-ask. It leads to a conversation about whose budget the purchase will come from and who else within their company holds the power to torpedo the deal.

Often, you'll find yourself talking to someone other than the budget owner. Your future pitches will hit unseen snags unless you learn who else matters and what they care about. This knowledge of their purchasing process will eventually turn into a repeatable sales roadmap.

"Who else should I talk to?"

Good question. Yes! End every conversation like this. Lining up the first few conversations can be challenging, but if you're onto something interesting and treating people well, your leads will quickly multiply via intros.

If someone doesn't want to make intros, that's cool too. Just leave them be. You've learned that you're either screwing up the meeting (probably by being too formal, pitchy, or clingy) or they don't actually care about the problem you're solving. Take anything nice they say with an extra grain of salt.

"Is there anything else I should have asked?"

Good question. Usually, by the end of the meeting, people understand what you're trying to do. Since you don't know the industry, they'll often be sitting there quietly while you completely miss the most important point.

Asking this question gives them a chance to politely "fix" your line of questioning. And they will!

This question is a bit of a crutch: you'll discard it as you get better at asking good questions and as you get to know the industry.

Rule of thumb: People want to help you. Give them an excuse to do so.

USING THE MOM TEST

You'll notice that none of the good questions were about asking what you should build. One of the recurring "criticisms" about talking to customers is that you're abdicating your creative vision and building your product by committee. Given that people don't know what they want, that wouldn't be a terribly effective approach. Deciding what to build is your job.

The questions to ask are about your customers' lives: their problems, cares, constraints, and goals. You humbly and honestly gather as much information about them as you can and then take your own visionary leap to a solution. Once you've taken the leap, you confirm that it's correct (and refine it) through Commitment & Advancement, which we'll look at in Chapter 5.

It boils down to this: you aren't allowed to tell them what their problem is, and in return, they aren't allowed to tell you what to build. They own the problem, you own the solution.

Before we move on to confirming that you're building the right product, let's look at spotting and fixing some of the ways conversations go wrong.

CHAPTER 2

AVOIDING BAD DATA

Practically everyone I've seen talk to customers (including myself) has been giving themselves bad information. You probably are too. Bad data gives us false negatives (thinking the idea is dead when it's not) and—more dangerously—false positives (convincing yourself you're right when you're not).

There are three types of bad data:

1. Compliments
2. Fluff (generics, hypotheticals, and the future)
3. Ideas

Sometimes we invite the bad data ourselves by asking the wrong questions, but even when you try to follow The Mom Test, conversations still go off track. It could happen because you got excited and started pitching; because you had to talk about your idea to explain the reason for the meeting; or because the conversation is just stuck in hypothetical la-la-land.

These things happen. Once you start to notice, it's easy to get back on track by deflecting compliments, anchoring fluff, and digging beneath ideas.

DEFLECTING COMPLIMENTS

Most of your meetings will end with a compliment. It feels good. They said they liked it!

Unfortunately, they're almost certainly lying. Not necessarily intentionally. They might want to be supportive or to protect your feelings. Or your excitement might be rubbing off on them.

Even if they really *do* like it, that data is still worthless. For example, venture capitalists (professional judges of the future) are wrong far more than right. If even a VC's opinion is probably wrong, what weight could that of some random guy's possibly have?

With the exception of industry experts who have built very similar businesses, opinions are worthless. You want facts and commitments, not compliments.

The best way to escape the misinformation of compliments is to avoid them completely by not mentioning your idea. If they happen anyway, you need to deflect the compliment and get on with the business of gathering facts and commitments.

Before we look at how to properly deflect compliments, here's what happens when you take them at face value:

A bad conversation:

> You: "...And that's it. It's like X for Y, but better because of Z." *Bam! Totally nailed that pitch.*
>
> Them: "That's cool. Love it." *How is this relevant to me? (Compliment)*

You: "It's going to totally change the way you work. We're predicting cost savings of 35%." *I am so great.*

Them: "Sounds terrific. Keep me in the loop." *I can't believe I keep agreeing to these startup pitches. (Compliment + stalling tactic)*

You: "Awesome, thanks." *I'm just like Steve Jobs. Except more handsome.*

You: (Back at the office) "That meeting went really well. They said they loved it! In fact, everybody loves it. I really think we've finally found our big idea. We've found something people want." *It's margarita time!*

Your Team: (6 months later) "Why do we have zero customers? I thought you said everybody loved it?" *Wasn't this your job?*

You: "I don't know, I talked to like a thousand people. I must have missed one of their buying criteria. Don't worry, I'll go talk to them some more and we'll get it next time." *Doooooomed.*

Let's try that again while properly deflecting the confounding compliments.

A good conversation:

You: "...And that's it. It's like X for Y, but better because of Z." *Rats, I just slipped into pitch mode. Let's try to recover this and learn something.*

Them: "That's really cool. I love it." *How is this even relevant to me?* (*Compliment*)

You: "Whoops — really sorry about that — I got excited and started pitching. Listen: you guys seem to be doing a good job in this space — do you mind if I ask how you're dealing with this stuff at the moment?" *That compliment made me suspicious. Let's deflect it and find out whether they're a potential customer or are just trying to get rid of me.*

Them: "What? Oh, well, sure. We've got a couple people who manage the process just to make sure we're all in sync, and then we use Excel and a lot of emails to keep it all moving. Anyway, I really like your idea. I'm sure it will do well." *If you want facts, here they are, but your idea still isn't a good fit for me and there's no way I'm going to express an interest in buying* (*notice the sneaky compliment at the end*).

You: "I haven't heard of anyone solving it quite like that — that's interesting. Can you talk me through how it actually all fits together?" *Let's ignore & deflect that compliment to focus on the fact that they're spending a lot of money to solve this. Two full time staff!? We never suspected it was worth this much.*

Them: (More delicious workflow data)

You: "What sort of difficulties have come up with doing

that?" *This is a bit generic and isn't the world's greatest question, but I'm trying to find an anchor to learn about workflow inefficiencies and bumps. When I find one, I'll dig around that signal with more follow-ups.*

Them: (Even more workflow and alternate solution data)

If we're early in the learning process, the meeting could end here quite happily. We have the learning we came for. If we're slightly later-stage and already have a product, we might continue by zooming in and pushing for commitments or sales.

Remember though: you don't need to end up with what you wanted to hear in order to have a good conversation. You just need to get to the truth. Here's a good conversation with a solid negative result.

A good (negative) conversation:

Them: "That's really cool. I love it." *Compliment.*

You: "How are you dealing with this stuff at the moment?" *Deflect that compliment and get to the real facts.*

Them: "Oh, it's really not that big of a deal. We kind of just ignore it." *The implications of the problem are non-existent so I'm not in the market for a solution.*

You can always be happy with a conversation like the above. You saw through the false compliment and found the facts behind the mirage. If the conversation is friendly, I might ask them to talk me through their process anyway so I can try to figure out whether it's an industry-wide non-problem or something specific to them.

Did you notice that in the conversations above, practically every response contains a sneaky compliment? They are pervasive, constantly trying to trick us into thinking the meeting "went well".

Ignoring compliments should be easy, but it's not. We crave validation and, as such, are often tricked into registering compliments as reliable data instead of vacuous fibs. Sometimes it's easier to spot the symptoms than to notice the sneaky compliment itself.

Symptoms (in the meeting):

- "Thanks!"
- "I'm glad you like it."

Symptoms (back at the office):

- "That meeting went really well."
- "We're getting a lot of positive feedback."
- "Everybody I've talked to loves the idea."

All of these are warning signs. If you catch yourself or your teammates saying something like this, try to get specific. Why did that person like the idea? How much money would it save him? How would it fit into his life? What else has he tried? If you don't know, then you've got a compliment instead of real data.

Rule of thumb: Compliments are the fool's gold of customer learning: shiny, distracting, and worthless.

ANCHORING FLUFF

Fluff comes in 3 cuddly shapes:

- Generic claims ("I usually", "I always", "I never")
- Future-tense promises ("I would", "I will")
- Hypothetical maybes ("I might", "I could")

When someone starts talking about what they "always" or "usually" or "never" or "would" do, they are giving you generic and hypothetical fluff. Ask good questions that obey The Mom Test to anchor them back to specifics in the past. Ask when it last happened or for them to talk you through it. Ask how they solved it and what else they tried.

The world's most deadly fluff is: "I would definitely buy that."

It just sounds so *concrete*. As a founder, you desperately want to believe it's money in the bank. But folks are wildly optimistic about what they would do in the future. They're always more positive, excited, and willing to pay in the imagined future than they are once that future arrives.

The first startup I worked at fell for the "I would definitely buy that" trap and subsequently lost about 10 million bucks. They mistook fluffy future promises and excited compliments for commitment. They incorrectly believed they had proven themselves right and wildly over-invested.

The worst type of fluff-inducing question you can ask is, "Would you ever?" Of course they *might*. Someday. That doesn't mean they will. Other fluff-inducing questions include:

- "Do you ever..."
- "Would you ever..."
- "What do you usually..."
- "Do you think you..."
- "Might you..."
- "Could you see yourself..."

You don't need to avoid these questions 100% of the time. They aren't exactly toxic. It's just that the responses are useless. The mistake is in valuing the answers, not in asking the questions. In fact, sometimes these questions can help you transition into more concrete questioning.

Transitioning from a fluffy question to a concrete one:

You: "Do you ever X?" *A fluff-inducing question.*

Them: "Oh yeah, all the time." *A fluffy answer which has no value in itself, but which we can anchor from.*

You: "When's the last time that happened?" *We use The Mom Test and ask for a concrete example in the past.*

Them: "Two weekends ago." *We've successfully anchored the fluff and are now ready to get real facts instead of generics and hypotheticals.*

You: "Can you talk me through that?" *Back to asking good questions.*

To use a more tangible example, let's say you're designing some sort of inbox management tool:

A good conversation, anchoring generic fluff:

Them: "I'm an 'Inbox 0' zealot. It's totally changed my life." *A generic (e.g. fluffy) claim.*

You: "Haha, nice. I'm an 'Inbox 0' failure. What's your inbox at right now?" *Let's get specific to see if this fluff holds up.*

Them: "Looks like about ten that have come in since this morning." *Facts!*

You: "Okay wow, so you are on top of things. I have like 200 right now. When's the last time it totally fell apart for you?" *He's still claiming to be on top of his email, so I'm going to look for concrete examples where he wasn't.*

Them: "Ug, 3 weeks ago. I was travelling and the internet at the hotel totally didn't work. It took me like 10 days to get back on track."

You: "Can you talk me through how you handled it?" *Successfully anchored — now we're talking about what actually happens instead of what "usually" happens.*

In this case, we took the generic claim, "My inbox is always under control" and added the important caveat: "Except when it's not, in which case it's a total nightmare to recover from." While using generics, people describe themselves as who they want to be, not who they actually are. You need to get specific to bring out the edge cases.

Let's say you're building a mobile loyalty app to help stores give deals and discounts to their most loyal customers and you hear the guy in line in front of you complaining:

A bad conversation (pitching and accepting fluff):

> Them: "Which idiot decided it was a good idea to make me carry around a thousand cafe loyalty cards?"
>
> You: "Ohmygosh hi! I just so happen to be building a mobile app to help stores give out discounts to their most loyal customers so you'd never need to carry paper cards again. Do you think you would use something like that?" *This is pretty much as bad of a question as you can find. You've revealed your ego and asked a "would you ever" question. You're begging for a false positive.*
>
> Them: "Heck yes, it's about time! I would definitely use that." *Fluffy, hypothetical, future promise.*

By switching into pitch mode, we just wasted a perfectly good opportunity for learning and instead got a fistful of fluff. Let's try again.

A good conversation:

> Them: "What idiot decided it was a good idea to make me carry around a thousand cafe loyalty cards?"

You: "It's crazy, right? My wallet is like two feet thick. Hey, have you ever tried any of those loyalty apps for your phone?" *Anchor to past behaviours.*

Them: "Those exist?" *Perhaps my rage is misplaced.*

You: "Yeah, I'm sure you've seen the little signs for that one in the campus cafe."

Them: "Oh yeah, I remember. I'm always kind of in a rush, though." *This is a nice bit of customer insight about their state of mind and circumstances when you're trying to advertise to them.*

You: "Why don't you download it now?" *If someone's being flaky, put them to a decision. If they don't care enough to try solving their problem today, they aren't going to care about your solution tomorrow.*

Them: "I'll do it next time." *Not a real problem.*

You can't help but laugh when you overhear these exchanges. "Someone should definitely make an X!" "Have you looked for an X?" "No, why?" "There are like 10 different kinds of X." "Well, I didn't really need it anyway."

Long story short, that person is a complainer, not a customer. They're stuck in the la-la-land of imagining they're the sort of person who finds clever ways to solve the petty annoyances of their day.

Beyond rousting some poor soul's consumeristic hypocrisy, anchoring the fluff can yield useful signals:

> You: "...Have you ever tried any of those loyalty apps for your phone?"

> Them: "Yeah, I downloaded a couple of them. You need a different one for every chain. I don't want a hundred apps clogging up my phone any more than I want a bunch of cards in my wallet."

So he's an actively searching potential user, but we'd need to get critical mass with retailers before he'll be happy. Maybe we could take over a small university town first. Or he might say:

> Them: "I looked into it, but you only end up getting like a 10% discount. That seems less like a loyalty reward and more like a cheap way for them to collect a bunch of data about me."

So he was on the fence, but needs better perks. Maybe we could find a way to force merchants into deeper discounts like Groupon was able to do. He also has privacy concerns. Or he could respond with:

> Them: "Have you ever actually tried using that app? It's abysmal. It takes longer to find the stupid button than to buy my coffee."

So all we need to do (for this particular user) is to out-execute and simplify.

The list goes on. There are tons of useful responses you can get. Even learning that the person is a non-customer is useful. To move toward this truth, you just need to reject their generic claims, incidental complaints, and fluffy promises. Instead, anchor them on the life they already lead and the actions they're already taking.

DIGGING BENEATH IDEAS

Entrepreneurs are always drowning in ideas. We have too many ideas, not too few. Still, folks adore giving us more. At some point during a good conversation, the person you're talking to may "flip" to your side of the table. This is good news. They are excited and see the potential, so they'll start listing tons of ideas, possibilities and feature requests.

Write them down, but don't rush to add them to your todo list. Startups are about focusing and executing on a single, scalable idea rather than jumping on every good one which crosses your desk.

Let's say you're mid-conversation when this idea drops:

> Them: "Are you guys going to be able to sync to Excel? I really think that's the killer feature."

What do you do here? The *wrong* response is to write "sync to Excel" on your todo list and then move on. That's the fast-lane to feature-creep. Instead, take a moment to dig into the motivations behind the request.

> You: "What would syncing to Excel allow you to do?" *Maybe there's an easier way I can help you achieve the same thing.*

> Them: "We've got all these legacy reports and we need to go through them every now and then. It would be nice to have everything in one place, you know?" *Don't worry, it's not a key buying criteria.*

Or they might say:

Them: "We've tried a bunch of these things and it's always the syncing that kills it." *They're actively searching for solutions which are all missing a must-have feature — this could be your major differentiator.*

Or:

Them: "We have a decent workaround, as you saw. But it takes nearly a week at the end of each month to pull all the reports together. It's a big pain and totally stalls our work." *They've cobbled together a home-brew solution, know it's costing them money, and are ideally suited to become an early customer.*

At my first company Habit, when we were starting to sell our product to enterprise companies, MTV said that they needed analytics and reports for their campaigns. I made a big mistake by accepting the feature request and face value and beginning the next meeting with a demo of our shiny new analytics dashboard (custom-built to solve their request, of course). They "ooh'ed" and "ahh'ed" appropriately and I left thinking we'd nailed it. We'd built in a zillion options and it could carve up your data every which way. It was technically and aesthetically lovely.

Unfortunately, 90% of what we had built was irrelevant. We just didn't know that yet.

They started calling every Friday asking me to email over a CSV (data file) of the week's stats, so we added CSV export to the dashboard. Later, they asked for the report as a PDF instead of an CSV, so we obediently built PDF export. That took longer.

Salt was rubbed in the wound when, weeks later, they were *still* calling every Friday and asking me to export and send over the same stupid analytics report. And every week, I would do so while politely explaining that, you know, we built this awesome self-serve dashboard so they could have their data whenever they wanted. And then, the next Friday, they'd call.

It turned out we had entirely missed the real reason they'd been excited about our analytics demo. In fact, we'd missed their whole motivation for wanting analytics in the first place.

The memory of being burned by feature requests was still fresh in my mind when they asked if we could add their logo and colours to the reports. I asked a couple incredulous questions about why in the world they wanted this feature when they didn't even use the ones we had already built. I felt like an exasperated Dad at Christmas: "But you don't even play with the toys I bought for your birthday!"

So, I finally—and inadvertently—did the smart thing when I asked, "Why do you want this feature? What do branded reports get you that unbranded ones don't? It's the same data, right?" They replied, "Oh yeah, of course. I mean, nobody even reads these. Our clients just like to get something emailed to them at the end of every week and we think they'd be happier if it was a bit fancier, you know?" I knew exactly.

They had asked for analytics. We had jumped to the conclusion that they wanted to better understand their data. But they had really just wanted a way to keep their own clients happy. If we had properly understood that, we would have built a totally different (and much simpler) set of features.

Consider how much easier our lives would have been if we'd understood the motivation behind the request. Instead of enabling the exploration and export of all campaign data, we could have just always exported the few high-level numbers a big brand manager would be interested in. And instead of a self-serve dashboard, we could set up a little scheduler to send it to them every Friday. In fact, we didn't even need to build a dashboard.

And instead of coding up a layout and branding system for the reports, we could have had an intern hand-build them each week. All wasted because I didn't ask the right question. Wish I had those 3 months back!

When you hear a request, it's your job to understand the motivations which led to it. You do that by digging around the question to find the root cause. Why do they bother doing it this way? Why do they want the feature? How are they currently coping without the feature? Dig.

You should dig in the same way around emotional signals to understand where they're coming from. Just like feature requests, any strong emotion is worth exploring. Is someone angry? Dig. Embarrassed? Dig. Overjoyed? Dig!

I once overheard a founder interviewing someone at a cafe table next to me. The founder mentioned a problem and the guy responded, "Yeah, that's pretty much the worst part of my day." The founder jotted something down in his notebook, and then *moved on to the next question.* What!? It's the worst part of his day and you're not going to figure out why? That's insane. You've got to dig.

Questions to dig into feature requests:

- "Why do you want that?"
- "What would that let you do?"
- "How are you coping without it?"
- "Do you think we should push back the launch to add that feature, or is it something we could add later?"
- "How would that fit into your day?"

Questions to dig into emotional signals:

- "Tell me more about that."
- "That seems to really bug you — I bet there's a story here."
- "What makes it so awful?"
- "Why haven't you been able to fix this already?"
- "You seem pretty excited about that — it's a big deal?"
- "Why so happy?"
- "Go on."

These nudges don't need to be complicated. People love talking about their opinions and emotions. Digging into a signal is basically just giving them permission to do a brain dump.

Rule of thumb: Ideas and feature requests should be understood, but not obeyed.

AVOIDING APPROVAL-SEEKING

As we've seen, compliments are dangerous and sneaky. So if we can nip them in the bud before they bloom, so much the better. The main source of compliment-creation is seeking approval, either intentionally or inadvertently.

Doing it intentionally is fishing for compliments. In other words, you aren't really looking for contradictory information. You've already made up your mind, but need someone's blessing to take the leap.

Symptoms of Fishing For Compliments:

- "I'm thinking of starting a business... so, do you think it will work?"
- "I had an awesome idea for an app — do you like it?"

Accidental approval-seeking is what I call "The Pathos Problem." It happens when you expose your ego, leading people to feel they ought to protect you by saying nice things.

This comes up when you tell someone about an idea you obviously care about (which is pretty much always, since otherwise you wouldn't be asking). Even if you give folks permission to be honest and ask for criticism, they're still going to pull their punches.

Symptoms of The Pathos Problem:

- "So here's that top-secret project I quit my job for... what do you think?"
- "I can take it — be honest and tell me what you really think!"

To deal with The Pathos Problem, keep the conversation focused on the other person and ask about specific, concrete cases and examples. Once someone detects that your ego is on the line, they'll give you fluffy mis-truths and extra compliments. Disregard that data and use The Mom Test to re-focus on the person, their life, and their goals. Folks tend not to lie about specific stuff that's already happened, regardless of your ego.

Some famous entrepreneurs don't suffer the effects of The Pathos Problem, but you should ignore their advice since it's not reproducible if you aren't them. Guys like Elon Musk, Reid Hoffman, and Gordon Ramsey are all notorious for actively seeking negative feedback. It evidently works for them. But nobody is worried about hurting Elon, Reid, or Gordon's feelings. You and I must be more circumspect.

In short, remember that compliments are worthless and people's approval doesn't make your business better. Keep your idea and your ego out of the conversation until you're ready to ask for commitments.

Rule of thumb: If you've mentioned your idea, people will try to protect your feelings.

CUT OFF PITCHES

Being pitchy is the dark side of the "seeking approval" coin. Instead of inviting compliments by being vulnerable, you're demanding them by being annoying. It's when you hold someone hostage and won't let them leave until they've said they like your idea. Normally, compliments are well-intentioned. In this case, they're just trying to get you out of their office.

"Won't-take-no-for-an-answer" is generally a good quality for a founder to have. But when it creeps into a conversation that's meant to be about learning, it works against you.

Symptoms:

- "No no, I don't think you get it..."
- "Yes, but it also does this!"

If you slip into pitch mode, just apologise. You're excited about your idea. That's good! Otherwise you wouldn't have taken this crazy leap in the first place. But suddenly, you find yourself five minutes into an enthusiastic monologue while the other person nods politely. That's bad. Once you start talking about your idea, they stop talking about their problems. Cut yourself off and say something like:

> You: "Whoops—I just slipped into pitch mode. I'm really sorry about that—I get excited about these things. Can we jump back to what you were just saying? You were telling me that..."

If they say they really want to hear about what you're working on, promise that you'll tell them at the end of the meeting or loop them in for an early demo, and that you just want to talk a bit more about their stuff before biasing them with your idea.

Rule of thumb: Anyone will say your idea is great if you're annoying enough about it.

TALK LESS

You can't learn anything useful unless you're willing to spend a few minutes shutting up (even if you have something really smart to say).

After you introduce your idea (either intentionally or accidentally), they're going to begin a sentence with something like "So it's similar to..." or "I like it but..." You will be hugely tempted to interrupt and "fix" their understanding. Alternately, they'll raise a topic you have a really good answer to. For example, they'll mention how important security is, and you'll want to cut in and tell them you've thought about all that already. Both interruptions are mistakes.

In each case, the customer was about to give you a privileged glimpse into their mental model of the world. Losing that learning is a shame. You'll have the chance to fill them in later. Plus, it's annoying to people if they start trying to help you and you cut them off to correct them.

Rule of thumb: The more you're talking, the worse you're doing.

CHAPTER 3

ASKING IMPORTANT QUESTIONS

Once we know about The Mom Test and start trying to ask non-biasing questions, sometimes we over-compensate and ask completely trivial ones. Asking someone how old they are isn't biasing, but it also doesn't move your business forward. You have to apply The Mom Test to the questions which matter. Otherwise you're just spinning your wheels.

In addition to ensuring that you aren't asking trivialities, you also need to search out the world-rocking scary questions you've been unintentionally shrinking from. The best way to find them is with thought experiments. Imagine that the company has failed and ask why that happened. Then imagine it as a huge success and ask what had to be true to get there. Find ways to learn about those critical pieces.

You can tell it's an important question when its answer could completely change (or disprove) your business. If you get an unexpected answer to a question and it doesn't affect what you're doing, it wasn't a terribly important question to begin with.

Every time you talk to someone, you should be asking at least one question which has the potential to destroy your currently imagined business.

One of my companies had some legal ambiguities around content ownership. We were okay in theory, but lacked strong precedents. I was always a bit nervous we would get "found out." A key customer's execs were excited and their creatives were thrilled. We had even brought the stubborn tech team around to our side. But in all my early customer conversations, I never asked to talk to their lawyers. For whatever reason, that was an important question which I shrunk from, and not asking it cost us at least half a million bucks.

There's no easy solution to making yourself face and ask these questions. I once heard the general life advice that, for unpleasant tasks, you should imagine what you would have someone else do if you were delegating it. Then do that. And remember, you're allowed to ask about money. You're a startup. It's okay.

Rule of thumb: You should be terrified of at least one of the questions you're asking in every conversation.

LOVE BAD NEWS

One of the reasons we avoid important question is because asking them is scary. It can bring us to the unsettling realisation that our beloved idea is fundamentally flawed. Or that the major client is never going to buy. Although this sort of news seems unfortunate, we need to learn to love it. It's solid learning and is getting us closer to the truth.

If you've only got one shot, then bad news is bad news. If your bungee jumping cord doesn't work, that's bad. If you've sunk your retirement savings into opening a cafe and it doesn't work, that's bad. If you hustle together $50k to start your business and spend all $50k on your first idea only to see it fail, that's bad.

On the other hand, if you have $50k and spend $5k to learn you're running down a dead end, that's awesome. You can use the rest to find a viable path to your goal, with the advantage of all the extra things you now know.

Similarly, if you have an exciting idea for a new product and go talk to a couple customers who don't actually care about it, then that's a great result. You just saved yourself however much time and money it would have cost to try building and selling it.

We go through the futile process of asking for opinions and fishing for compliments because we crave approval. We want to believe that the support and sign-off of someone we respect means our venture will succeed. But really, that person's opinion doesn't matter. They have no idea if the business is going to work. Only the market knows.

Learning that your beliefs are wrong is frustrating, but it's progress. It's bringing you ever closer to the truth of a real problem and a good market. The worst thing you can do is ignore the bad news while searching for some tiny grain of validation to celebrate. You want the truth, not a gold star.

Some of the most informative (and thus best) responses you can get are along the lines of, "Umm, I'm not so sure about that" and "That's pretty neat." Both are lukewarm responses which tell you they don't care.

In this context, "best" means learning, not selling. If you're a sales guy going door to door selling gadgets and someone doesn't care, then that is a bad result: you're not getting paid. But if you're trying to decide whether to invest your time and money in developing, building and promoting that gadget, then lukewarm is a terrific response. It gives you a crystal clear signal that this person does not care. It's reliable information you can take to the bank.

The classic error in response to a lukewarm signal is to "up your game" and pitch them until they say something nice. Unless they're holding a check, the only thing to gain from "convincing" them are false positives. You're not here to collect compliments; you're trying to learn the truth. Their lukewarm response already gave you that.

If they're still engaged in the conversation, it's worth asking a couple follow-up questions to understand the nature of their apathy. Is the "problem" not actually that big of a deal? Are they fundamentally different from your ideal customers? Do they not care about the specific implementation? Are they worn out and skeptical from hearing too many pitches, like cafe owners in the aftermath of Groupon? Are they just plain tired today?

After that, say a big thanks and leave them to their day. They've probably helped you more than the guy who said he loved it.

Rule of thumb: There's more reliable information in a "meh" than a "Wow!" You can't build a business on a lukewarm response.

LOOK BEFORE YOU ZOOM

Another way to miss the important questions is by obsessing over ultimately unimportant nuances. We let ourselves get stuck in the details before understanding the big picture.

Everyone has problems they know about, but don't actually care enough about to fix. And if you zoom in too quickly and lead them to that semi-problem, they'll happily drown you in all the unimportant details. Zooming in too quickly on a super-specific problem before you understand the rest of the customers life can irreparably confuse your learnings.

A (really, really) bad conversation:

You: "Hi. Thanks for taking the time. We're building phone and tablet apps to help people stay in shape and just wanted to understand how you stay fit." *This isn't a terrible opening, but I'd generally avoid mentioning the idea unless I have to, since it does bias them.*

Them: "Okay." *I never exercise, so this should be quick.*

You: "How often do you go to the gym?" *This sort of demographic data doesn't give you any new insight, but can be useful for figuring out what sort of person you're talking to so you can ask relevant follow-ups.*

Them: "Not really ever." *Well, looks like we're done here then!*

You: "What would you say is your biggest problem with going to the gym?" *This is where the conversation goes horribly wrong. Instead of figuring out whether staying fit is actually a real problem, we're prematurely zooming in on it. Any response we get is going to be dangerously misleading.*

Them: "I guess the time it takes to get there. I'm always kind of busy, you know?" *Wait, who says I have a problem with going to the gym? I thought I just told you I don't care about the gym! But if I had to choose one, I guess I'd go with convenience. Not that I've done a pushup in 5 years. Pushups are pretty convenient.*

You: "Perfect. That's great. And could you rank these 4

in terms of which is most important to you in a fitness program: convenience, personalisation, novelty, or cost?" *Note that we're still assuming we're talking to a person who actually cares about getting in shape. Questions like this don't actually tell you if the person cares about any of it at all.*

Them: "Probably convenience, then cost, then personalisation, then novelty." *Since you asked, I'll answer. Hypothetically speaking, of course.*

You: "Okay. Awesome. Thanks so much. We're working on an app to help you exercise in the convenience of your own home. I think it's going to be a great fit for what you care about." *Totally missing the point and mis-interpreting the conversation as validation. Now fishing for compliments.*

Them: "Cool. I'd love to try it when it launches." *Half-hearted compliment plus non-committal stalling tactic.*

You: "Great — I'll send over one of our beta keys so you can check it out." *We got a user!*

Them: "Thanks." *I am literally never going to type that in.*

The reason this conversation is so very bad is because, if you aren't paying attention, it seems like it went well. When you zoom in too quickly on one problem area, you can think you've validated a "top" problem when you haven't. You just led them there.

If you ask me what's my biggest problem with staying fit, I'll probably tell you it's the time cost of going to the gym. Because I know I'm supposed to say something. But then, if you build me a workout-at-home app, I'm going to ignore it. Even though commute time is the *biggest* problem with getting in shape, the whole area of fitness just isn't something I care about enough to act on. My #1 fitness problem is still an unimportant one.

Let's start the conversation again and fix it when it starts to go off track. You can

A good conversation:

You: "How often do you go to the gym?"

Them: "Um. Not really ever." *Looks like we're done here.*

You: "Why not?" *Instead of taking for granted that staying fit is one of their top priorities, let's dig into the motivations.*

Them: "I don't know, it's just not something I'm that worried about, you know?" *Not trying to fix this, so unlikely to buy or use an app.*

You: "When's the last time you did try? Have you ever joined a gym or taken up jogging or anything?" *Let's anchor the generic just to make sure...*

Them: "Oh yeah, I used to be into sports in high school. It just hasn't been a big deal since I settled down. Running around after the kids gives me all the cardio I need!"

> You: "Haha, gotcha. Thanks for the time!" *This was a pleasant conversation and we learned what we came for, so we can abandon ship and leave him to his day.*

The premature zoom is a real problem because it leads to data which seems like validation, but is actually worthless. In other words, it's a big source of false positives.

Let's re-run the same conversation, but instead of immediately zooming in on exercise, we'll start more generic, since we aren't sure that fitness is a must-solve problem:

A good conversation:

> You: "What are your big goals and focuses right now?" *Products which solve problems on this list are infinitely more likely to get bought. We might alternately ask for major annoyances, costs, or joys.*

> Them: "The big one is finalising that promotion at work. And we just bought our first house, so I've got to get that all fixed up and ready to go. Exciting times. And I want to find a bit more time for the missus, you know? Things have been pretty busy lately." *Work, house, and marriage. Not looking good for us!*

> You: "You're buying a new house and expect to be *less* busy?"

> Them: "Can't blame a guy for hoping."

> You: "Is getting healthier on that list?" *We probably already know the answer, but it doesn't hurt to ask leading*

> *questions when you're about to abort the conversation anyway. If they come back with a positive, just be a little extra careful in making sure they aren't lying.*

> Them: "I'm actually feeling pretty good at the moment." *Not a customer.*

We don't always need to start the conversation from square one of "do they care at all?" Sometimes we already know the problem exists as a top priority and we can safely zoom in immediately.

For example, let's say we help drive qualified leads to small business websites. We know that marketing is always a top 3 problem for small businesses, so we can focus on it and start the conversation by zooming in with a question like:

> You: What are your big problems with marketing? *We can safely zoom in on the problem of marketing since we're pretty much 100% certain it's a must-solve problem that people are ready to pay for.*

> Versus:

> You: What are your big problems right now? *If we aren't sure it's a must-solve problem, we can start more generic to see if they care enough about the problem category to mention it unprompted.*

Now imagine you've built the aforementioned marketing tool for small businesses and realise it could also be used to help bloggers get more attention. You're wondering if you have another strong customer segment. However, since blogs have a harder time monetising traffic than small businesses, we can't necessarily assume that they're also going to happily pay for traffic.

For example, I have a blog which I quite like (but which I don't take seriously as a business). If you're talking to me and you ask, "Hey Rob, what are your top problems with *marketing* your blog?" Then you've just prematurely zoomed in on a non-problem.

I'm going to tell you some sort of answer which sounds legit but is actually misleading. I might say that my keywords are all kind of generic, so it's hard to attract the right people. Or that I walk a fine line between writing beginner and advanced articles, so choosing the right topics is always weird. Whatever. Problems exist with my blog marketing, but the whole space just isn't something I'm too fussed about. I blog because it's fun, not because it pays my rent.

To have a useful conversation, you need to zoom back out to ask about my blog in general, rather than marketing my blog.

A good conversation:

> You: "Hey Rob, what are the top problems with your blog?"
>
> Me: "I'm grumpy that Google Reader disappeared — I lost like half my followers. And this book is consuming all of my interest in writing, so I haven't really posted in months. And Wordpress seems so slow these days." *Of the topics here, one of them (Google Reader and audience size) is related to marketing, so you can anchor on that and figure out whether I'm a customer or just a complainer.*
>
> You: "That Google Reader thing is a mess. What are you

doing about it?" *Now that you've let me raise the topic, you know it's on my mind and can more safely zoom in to talk about that specifically. As before, try to figure out what I'm already spending time and money on.*

Me: "Nothing, really. I don't know what to do. But it sucks." *I'm not appearing terribly motivated, but the fact that I don't know what to do could give you hope.*

You: "Have you looked into what your options are?" *Continue anchoring and digging.*

Me: "No, I just caught the drama on Hacker News." *I knew the reader-pocalypse was coming and didn't even search around to properly understand the implications and my options. This just isn't a big deal for me, despite how "annoyed" I claim to be.*

You: "Are you spending a lot of time working to build your audience back up?" *You are digging into the audience size signal, since it's relevant to your space. This is a fluff-inviting question (hypothetical future-tense), so you should be skeptical of the answer, but it's hard to see a better way to get at the information you want from here. Not every question can be perfect, sadly.*

Me: "Probably just keep on writing when I have something to say. It's more of a hobby than a business, really."

At this point, you might be suspicious about how much I actually care about my blog. When it's not clear whether a problem is a must-solve-right-now (e.g. you're selling a painkiller) or a nice-to-have (you're selling a vitamin), you can get some clarity by asking cost/value questions like the following.

"Does-this-problem-matter" questions:

- "How seriously do you take your blog?"
- "Do you make money from it?"
- "Have you tried making more money from it?"
- "How much time do you spend on it each week?"
- "Do you have any major aspirations for your blog?"
- "Which tools and services do you use for it?"
- "What are you already doing to improve this?"
- "What are the 3 big things you're trying to fix or improve right now?"

Some of these questions are generic, but give us signals that we can anchor on and dig around. The bulk of them are about finding out whether the person we're talking to is taking this space seriously. Are they spending money? Making money? Is the problem in their top 3? Are they actively looking for solutions?

When you fall into a premature zoom, you can waste a ton of time figuring out the minutia of a trivial problem. Even if you learn everything there is to know about that particular problem, you still haven't got a business.

Rule of thumb: Start broad and don't zoom in until you've found a strong signal, both with your whole business and with every conversation.

GAZE UPON THE ELEPHANT

Sometimes we comfort ourselves by asking questions which don't actually de-risk the business or resolve those critical, big, scary, lurking questions. We ignore the elephant in the room.

Let's say we suspect that teachers from the poorest schools are completely overloaded, and that our tools would save them time so they could better educate their students. We go talk to them and confirm that yes, they are completely overloaded. We then spend weeks with them, figuring out exactly what their dream tool would do. Unfortunately, we've missed the elephant, which is that the poorest schools may not have the budgets available to pay us what we need to sustain and grow a business. We're liable to spend a huge amount of time exploring a real and urgent problem, only to hop into the deadpool due to our customer's budgeting issues.

Startups tend to have multiple failure points (e.g. the problems of the teachers and the ability of the schools to pay us). If any of these conditions doesn't exist, we must overhaul our idea. It's tempting to obsess over the most interesting of several failure points and ignore the others. And then we miss important questions.

Beyond the risks of our customers and market, we also have challenges with our own product. Overlooking product risks is just as deadly as overlooking the goals and constraints of our customers. Take the following conversation with a professional public speaker. Is it full of good data or bad data?

An ambiguous conversation:

Them: "...I get paid 2 or 3 grand per talk. Sometimes

more if it's corporate work." *Some good pricing and value signals.*

You: "Where do you get your gigs? Do you have an agent?" *Trying to understand the alternatives.*

Them: "Yeah. He kind of sucks though. Most of my work comes through people who just know me from my blog or have seen my other talks." *Hardly a must-solve problem since he has a reliable workaround, but at least it's high value.*

You: "What's wrong with the agent? And why do you still work with him?" *Dig.*

Them: "I'm one of the lowest-paid people they work with, so I get ignored a lot. But sometimes he brings in deals, so whatever. It's free money." *Good information on his motivations and goals.*

At this point, let's say I'm confident that getting gigs is important to him. I also know what it's worth and how he's currently accomplishing it. So I zoom in to introduce the problem I'm solving and the way I want to approach it.

You: "I'm building a marketplace to cut out the agents and connect event organisers directly with speakers. It should help you get more gigs and keep the agent fees. How would that fit into your speaking life?"

Them: "Man, that's awesome. If you could get me more more gigs — or better paid ones — I'd happily drop my agent and pay you 20% of the boost. I know a bunch of other people who would love to as well." *This is the important bit — is it good?*

So what's the result? Beyond being excited, we got some concrete data about how valuable this could be to him. Plus, he gave a verbal commitment to be one of our early users. It sure *seems* good.

But what did he actually tell us? He said that *if* we can get him more gigs, *then* he'll pay a cut. Well, obviously. Who doesn't want free money? His needs are clear: he wants to make more money by speaking. If we can send him work, he'll share some of it with us. This was never really in doubt.

The phrase "if you could get me more gigs" is basically shifting the burden from the customer to your product. Even though you've found a pain, your success is dependent on a bunch of other factors, such as your ability to grow a healthy supply of paying gigs which are a good fit for him. Will you be able to do that? It remains to be seen.

This situation is easier to spot in the online advertising industry. Imagine running customer conversations with an advertiser to try to understand their pains so you can convince them to advertise on your site. They'd sort of look at you blankly and say, "Listen, if you can get enough page views, we'll pay you for them." In fact, it's such a well established would-pay-to-solve-problem that you don't even need to talk to them to set it up. You just plug in an ad network and you're done.

Same deal with affiliate commissions. If you sell a company's products, you get a cut. That's just how it works. You don't need to explore or validate or understand their problems. The risk resides in your ability to get lots of traffic and sell lots of products. If you can, they'll pay you.

In all of these examples, the risk is in your product, not in the customer. They'll pay if your product gets big enough.

- Product risk — Can I build it? Can I grow it?
- Customer/market risk — Do they want it? Will they pay me? Are there lots of them?

You can't overlook either one. I remember talking to a founder who had wasted 3 months on worthless customer conversations. He wanted to start a company building gadgets that tracked the fertility of farm animals, ultimately boosting birthrates and thus farm revenue. When he talked to farmers, he asked questions like, "Would you switch trackers if something cheaper and more effective was available?" That's the same as asking someone whether they would like more money. The farmers responded along the lines of, "If you can build what you say you can build, I'll equip my whole herd." The problem is, he couldn't build it. The risk was in the product.

I've also seen this strike several of the recent companies who want to use mobile/realtime deals to drive foot traffic to bars and clubs. They run customer conversations with bar owners who confirm that: yes, they would like more customers on the slow nights; and yes, they would pay you if you could send customers on demand. The founders take this as strong validation ("They have the problem and committed to pay!") without recognising that the vast majority of the risk is in the product, not the market. Bars will pay, but only if you can amass a huge audience of consumers. Then the founders talk to consumers and ask if they would use an app which always pointed them to booming parties with cheap booze. Again, obviously yes. But that doesn't tell us whether we can actually achieve that critical mass of users.

Video games are pure product risk. What sort of question could you ask to validate your game idea? "Do you like having fun? Would you like to have *even more* fun?" Practically 100% of the risk is in the product and almost none is in the customer. You know people buy games. If yours is good and you can find a way to make them notice it, they'll buy it. You don't need to rediscover people's desire to play video games.

This isn't to say that you shouldn't talk to anyone if you're building something with product risk. In the case of the farm fertility monitor, it's good to know that the farmer isn't opposed to switching tech, for example. For the nightclubs, it's good to know that they're at least theoretically willing to pay for promotion. It would be tragic to succeed at the hard work of creating the product or community only to learn nobody will pay for it.

What all this *does* mean is that if you've got heavy product risk (as opposed to pure market risk), then you're not going to be able to prove as much of your business through conversations alone. The conversations give you a starting point, but you'll have to start building product earlier and with less certainty than if you had pure market risk.

PREPARE YOUR LIST OF 3

Pre-plan the 3 most important things you want to learn from any given type of person (e.g. customers, investors, industry experts, key hires, etc). Update the list as your questions change.

Pre-planning your big questions makes it a lot easier to ask questions which pass The Mom Test and aren't biasing. It also makes it easier to face the questions that hurt. When we go through an unplanned conversation, we tend to focus on trivial stuff that keeps the conversation comfortable. Instead, decide on the tough questions in a calm environment with your team.

Your 3 questions will be different for each type of person you're talking to. If you have multiple types of customers or partners, have a list for each.

Don't stress too much about choosing the "right" important questions. They will change. Just choose whatever seems murkiest or most important *right now*. Answer those will give you firmer footing and a better sense of direction for your next 3.

You might get answers 1-3 from customer A, answer 4 from customer B, answers 5-7 from customer C. There's overlap and repetition, but you don't need to repeat the full set of questions with every participant. Your time is valuable; don't feel obliged to repeat questions you already have solid data on. Pick up where you left off and keep filling in the picture.

Knowing your list allows you to take better advantage of serendipitous encounters. Instead of running into that dream customer and asking to exchange business cards so you can "grab a coffee" (exactly like everyone else), you can just pop off your most important question. And that goes a long way toward keeping it casual (the advantages of which we'll discuss momentarily).

Rule of thumb: You always need a list of your 3 big questions.

CHAPTER 4
KEEPING IT CASUAL

By now, we know that zooming prematurely and introducing your idea too early creates biases and delivers bad data. In Steve Blank's original book on Customer Development, *4 Steps to the E.piphany*, he solves this by recommending 3 separate meetings: the first about the customer and their problem; the second about your solution; and the third to sell a product. By splitting the meetings, you avoid the premature zoom and Pathos Problem.

In practice, however, I've found it both difficult and inefficient to set up all 3 meetings. The time cost of a 1-hour meeting is more like 4 hours once you factor in the calendar dance, commuting, and reviewing. And it's a big time commitment to ask from the customer before you're in a position to show them anything in return.

In the early days, asking for the initial problem conversation was simply impossible for me. I wasn't credible enough, so nobody wanted to take a meeting just to talk to me about their day. Steve recommends starting with friendly first contacts. Definitely do that if you have them. When you ask questions that pass The Mom Test, the fact that they're friends won't bias your data.

In my case though, I was entering a new industry with high walls (brand advertising) and had no friendly first contacts.

As my credibility built after a couple years in the industry, I found myself able to get meetings without any real "reason". The 3-meeting structure was finally viable! But once I started doing it, it felt like a bad use of my time. The most precious resource in a startup is its founders' time. You have to put yourself where you matter most, and I wasn't finding early customer meetings to be that place. I wished I could get the learning without all the overhead.

If the solution isn't a 3-meeting series, then what is it? You may have noticed a trend throughout the conversation examples we've seen so far: keeping it casual.

Let's say I'm trying to build tools to help public speakers get more speaking gigs and I bump into one at a conference. I'm not going to try to set up a meeting. Instead, I'm just going to immediately transition into my most important question: "Hey, I'm curious—how did you end up getting this gig?" As a side bonus, we're also now having an interesting conversation and I'm far more likely to be remembered and get a meeting later.

When you strip all the formality from the process, you end up with no meetings, no "interviews", and a much easier time all around. The conversations become so fast and lightweight that you can go to a industry meetup and leave with a dozen customer conversations under your belt, each of which provided as much value as a lengthy formal meeting.

The structure of separate problem/solution/sales conversations is critical for avoiding bias, but it's important to realise that the first one doesn't actually need to be a meeting. It works better as a chat.

Rule of thumb: Learning about a customer and their problems works better as a quick and casual chat than a long, formal meeting.

THE MEETING ANTI-PATTERN

The Meeting Anti-Pattern is the tendency to relegate every opportunity for customer conversation into a calendar block.

Beyond being a bad use of your time and setting expectations that you're going to show them a product, over-reliance on formal meetings leads us to overlook perfectly good chances for serendipitous learning.

Imagine that you're in a crowded cafe, tapping away at your keyboard, when your dream boy/girl sits down next to you. They're wearing a charming hat and give you a friendly nod before cracking open a dog-eared old novel which just totally completes the mood. You slam down a quick espresso to psych yourself up and fumble through some sort of awkward monologue about how they seem like a really nice person and this is kind of weird because you don't even know each other but maybe they want to go get a coffee sometime? Like, a different coffee? At a different place?

It's obvious that this is a silly situation. After all, the purpose of a date is to talk to each other and see if you get along. Therefore, for all intents and purposes, you were already on one. And then you messed it up by trying to over-formalise it when you could have just chatted a bit and skipped that whole first date completely.

We're going to pull exactly the same trick on our early customer conversations. We're going to strip the pomp and circumstance and reduce it from a meeting to a chat. If we do it right, they won't even know we were talking about our idea.

I was once considering a product idea to make office managers more efficient. I played with the possibilities on

Friday, figured out the big questions over the weekend, and then went to an industry event on Monday. A handful of office managers were there and without any of them realising we'd "had a meeting", I'd learned that the big problem was really about debt collection rather than efficiency. I got there by just being interested and chatting with them over a beer: "X seems really annoying, how do you deal with it?" "Is Y as bad as it seems?" "You guys did a great job with Z... Where did you get that from?"

Being too formal is a crutch we use to deal with an admittedly ambiguous and awkward situation. Instead of leaving wiggle room for the unexpected, everything becomes a process. But there's a big time cost to formality, and it tends to clobber much of the learning we hoped to achieve.

Symptoms of formality:

- "So, first off, thanks for agreeing to this interview. I just have a few questions for you and then I'll let you get back to your day..."
- "On a scale of 1 to 5, how much would you say you..."

Learning from customers doesn't mean you have to be wearing a suit and sipping ominous boardroom coffee. Asking the right questions is fast and touches on topics that people find quite interesting. You can talk anywhere and save yourself the formal meetings until you have something concrete to show.

At their best, these conversations are a pleasure for both parties. You're probably the first person in a long time to be truly interested in the petty annoyances of their day.

Rule of thumb: If it feels like they're doing you a favour by talking to you, it's probably too formal.

HOW LONG ARE MEETINGS?

Early conversations are very fast. The chats grow longer as you move from the early broad questions ("Is this a real problem?") toward more specific product and industry issues ("Which other software do we have to integrate with to close the sale?")

For example, it only takes 5 minutes (maximum) to learn whether a problem exists and is important.

A bit further along, you'll find yourself asking questions which are answered with long stories explaining their workflow, how they spend their time, and what else they've tried. You can usually get what you came for in 10-15 minutes, but people love telling stories about themselves, so you can keep this conversation going indefinitely if it's valuable for you and fun for them.

At the extreme end, learning the details of an industry takes an hour or more. Thankfully, those are easier conversations to facilitate since the other person (usually some sort of industry expert) can go into a monologue once you point them in the right direction.

The duration of formal B2B meetings (the kind you schedule) is determined more by the arbitrary calendar block than by what you actually want to learn. Of course, you've liable to burn 15 minutes just to getting a cup of tea and saying hello before the meeting actually starts. But sometimes the tea is fancy, so that's nice.

Once you have a product and the meetings take on a more sales-oriented feel, you'll want to start carving out clear blocks of 30ish minutes. You might lose 5 minutes due to miscellaneous tardiness, spend 5 minutes saying hello, 5 minutes asking questions to understand their goals/problems/budget, 10 minutes to show/describe the product, and the last 5 minutes figuring out next steps and advancement. That's your half hour.

The potential speed of the early conversations is one of the big reasons I like keeping it casual and skipping the meeting. Scheduling and going to a meeting is too much overhead for a chat which only needs to be 10 minutes long. Even explaining that you're starting a company and would love to ask a couple questions can take 5 or 10 minutes. You'll make progress a lot faster if you're able to leave your idea out of it for as long as possible.

PUTTING IT TOGETHER

Even within a more formal meeting, you still might want to keep it casual if you're hoping to get non-biased feedback.

I once had a product idea to help busy investors to manage their dealflow. I knew they got hundreds of applications per month and figured it must be a spreadsheet nightmare. I lined up a couple meetings to ask about the industry. I showed up to the first meeting and, while making smalltalk, said something like "I was thinking, you guys must get a ton of leads, right?" The guy laughed and said that, yeah, it was crazy. I asked how in the world they deal with all that. He sort of shrugged and pointed at a cluster of about a dozen sticky notes on the wall.

Each held a name and a phone number. "Our analysts kill most of them before they ever reach us, and then we trash a bunch more. We only end up with a few that are serious contenders. Then we just call every couple weeks to see how it's going." I said it didn't sound so bad and he agreed that it works pretty well. And then he asked me what I wanted to talk about. But I didn't need anything else, because I'd learned what I came for: they don't have the problem.

That's successful learning. We disproved our idea before the guy even realised we were talking about it. It took 5 minutes, avoided biases, and didn't feed us any bad data in the form of compliments, fluff, or ideas. Instead, we got concrete facts about our customers which directly answer our most important questions.

Of course, it took a 2-hour commute to get to those 5 minutes. It can't be perfect every time.

Sometimes, as happened above, we prove ourselves wrong. Other times, everything we hear just makes us even more excited. In that case, we can stand atop all that we've learned and take the visionary leap of coming up with a specific offering to make our customers' lives better. And then we ask them to commit to it.

Rule of thumb: Give as little information as possible about your idea while still nudging the discussion in a useful direction.

CHAPTER 5

COMMITMENT AND ADVANCEMENT

Once we've learned the key facts about our industry and customers, it's time to zoom in again and start revealing our idea and showing some product. The bad news is that this invites nefarious compliments. The *good* news is that since we have the beginnings of a product, we're now in a position to cut through the false positives by asking for commitments.

In sales, moving the relationship to the next stage is called "advancement". It's like pushing a customer into the next step of your real-world acquisition funnel. They'll either move forward or make it clear that they're not a customer. Both are good results for your learning.

When you fail to push for advancement, you end up with zombie leads: potential customers (or investors) who keep taking meetings and saying nice things, but who never seem to cut a check. It's like your startup has been friend-zoned.

Thankfully, you caused it, and *that* means you can fix it. It's a consequence of being clingy and fearing rejection. By giving them a clear chance to either commit or reject it, you can get out of the friend-zone and identify the real leads.

As always, you're not trying to convince every person to like what you're doing. When you've got the information you came for (even if it's that they don't care), you can leave. But at some point, you do need to put them to a decision in order to get it.

Symptoms:

- A pipeline of zombie leads
- Product meetings that end with a compliment
- Product meetings that end with no clear next steps
- Meetings which "went well"
- They haven't given up anything of value

While a traditional sales guy might disagree with my definitions, for the sake of our context of customer learning, *commitment* and *advancement* are separate concepts which overlap quite a lot and tend to appear together.

- Commitment — They are showing they're serious by giving up something they value such as time, reputation, or money.
- Advancement — They are moving to the next step of your real-world funnel and getting closer purchasing.

Commitment and advancement often arrive hand-in-hand. For example, to move to the next step (advancement), you might need an introduction to your contact's boss (reputation commitment). As such, they are functionally equivalent for our purposes and I'm going to blur them into one concept for the following sections.

Rule of thumb: "Customers" who keep being friendly but aren't ever going to buy are a particularly dangerous source of mixed signals.

MEETINGS EITHER SUCCEED OR FAIL

It took me years to learn that there's no such thing as a meeting which just "went well". Every meeting either succeeds or fails. You've lost the meeting when you leave with a compliment or a stalling tactic. While we might spot something as blatant as "Let's talk again after the holidays... Don't call me, I'll call you," we accept the more subtle versions every day.

A meeting has succeeded when it ends with a commitment to advance to the next step. But you have to force this resolution or the meetings drift along in la-la-land while performing their ancient duty: wasting everyone's time.

If you leave with worthless wishy washiness, I'd bet you're falling for one (or both) of the following traps:

1. You're asking for their opinion about your idea (e.g. fishing for compliments)
2. You're not asking for a clear commitment or next steps

You know how to deal with compliments by now: deflect, ignore, and get back to business. Commitments are similarly easy to master, once we know what we're trying to do. When we leave without a commitment, sometimes it's because we asked and got rejected. That's sad, but it happens. Not everyone is going to convert and at least you now know where you stand. You have a strong negative data point. That's good learning!

The real failure is listed above as #2: not even asking. I never consider rejection to be a real failure. But not asking certainly is.

This can happen because you're avoiding the scary question or because you haven't figured out what the next steps should be.

Commitment is important. It shows us whether people actually care about what we're doing. The more they give up, the more we can trust them.

Rule of thumb: If you don't know what happens next after a product or sales meeting, the meeting was pointless.

THE CURRENCIES OF CONVERSATION

Commitment can be cash, but doesn't have to be. Think of it in terms of currency—what are they giving up for you? A compliment costs them nothing, so it's worth nothing and carries no data. The major currencies are time, reputation risk, and cash.

A time commitment could include:

- Clear next meeting with known goals
- Sitting down to give feedback on wireframes
- Using a trial of the product for a non-trivial period

Reputation risk commitments might be:

- Intro to peers or team
- Intro to a decision maker (boss, spouse, lawyer)
- Giving a public testimonial or case study

Financial commitments are easier to imagine and include:

- Letter of intent (non-legal but gentlemanly agreement to purchase)
- Pre-order
- Deposit

Strong commitments will often combine multiple currencies, such as someone agreeing to run a paid trial with their whole team, thus risking their time, money, and reputation.

Just like compliments aren't data when you're trying to learn about a problem, they also aren't progress when you're trying to validate a product. Hearing a compliment can still be useful though—it's a warning flag that the person you're talking to is trying to get rid of you.

Rule of thumb: The more they're giving up, the more seriously you can take what they're saying.

GOOD MEETING / BAD MEETING

Game time again. We just had a meeting. But how did it go? Was it a good meeting or a bad one? Why? And if it was bad, what can we do to fix it?

Have a think about the meetings listed below and then turn the page for further discussion.

"That's so cool. I love it!"
"Looks great. Let me know when it launches."
"There are a couple people I can intro you to when you're ready."
"What are the next steps?"

"I would definitely buy that."
"When can we start the trial?"
"Can I buy the prototype?"
"When can you come back to talk to the rest of the team?"

"That's so cool. I love it!"

Bad meeting. Pure, unadulterated compliment. This may make you feel good, but there is precisely zero data here. On the bright side, at least you won't hurt yourself on this one since it's so obviously fluff.

To fix it, deflect the compliment and get back to business.

"Looks great. Let me know when it launches."

Bad meeting. A compliment plus a stalling tactic is the classic way to end a pitch for something you're never going to buy. This comes in a lot of flavours, but they're all basically a polite way to say, "Don't call me, I'll call you."

The big error you can make here is to mistake this compliment-stall for a pre-order ("He said he'll buy it when it launches!"). To fix it, look for a commitment you can ask for today.

If you are very early stage, you might ask for an introduction to his boss or tech team or the budget-holder so you can "make sure you fully understand their needs." The point is just to find something to ask for that they are going to think twice about giving you.

If you were slightly further through development, you might push him to agree to be one of your alpha users and a case study for launch. If you've hit on a real problem, the customer jump at the chance to start making progress today and get early access.

"There are a couple people I can introduce you to when you're ready."

Nearly a good meeting, but right now it's bad. There's some data here, but probably not as much as you initially hope. At least you know he doesn't think you're completely nuts or he wouldn't have even made the fluffy offer (unless he's just name dropping). The problem is that the promise is so generic that it's a worthless signal.

To fix it, try to convert fuzzy promises into something more concrete. The more specific it is, the more seriously you can take it. For example: who does he want to introduce you to and what does "ready" mean? And why can't he make the intro now? This isn't about being pushy. You don't have manifest destiny over his rolodex. But you do need to distinguish between legitimate offers and polite gesturing. Knowing what "ready" means can also give you a better sense of your short-term goals.

"What are the next steps?"

Good meeting (usually). A classic good meeting conclusion. To succeed, a meeting doesn't need to end with a check in your pocket. It just needs to advance to the next step, whatever that is.

It's worth noting that you need to know your next steps to benefit from this. If you have to say, "Let me have a think about that and get back to you," then you've ruined a perfectly good meeting.

Of course, even clear next steps can be a lie. Everything can be a lie. But with next steps in your pocket, you've got a fighting chance. Keep an eye out for non-committal next steps such as to "think" or "check with the team" or "find a time to chat."

Although they may be sincere, it won't hurt to remain skeptical until the exchange of value actually happens.

"I would definitely buy that."

Bad meeting. Danger! There's admittedly some signal here, but the danger from false positives is off the charts. This is the misinterpreted "data" which sunk the first startup I worked at to the tune of ten million bucks.

To fix it, you need to shift from fuzzy future promises into concrete current commitments. For example, you could ask for a letter of intent, a pre-purchase, a deposit, or intros to other decision makers and team members. The reason Kickstarter is so wonderful is because it forces customers who say they would buy it to actually pull out a credit card and commit.

"When can we start the trial?"

Maybe a good meeting. Unlike "When does it launch," which is usually a stall, "When can we start" tends to be a step forward. Setting up new software and training staff is a big deal for most businesses. Even a "free" trial can cost them serious money. However, in some cases, "trying" software costs nothing, especially for individuals. For example, I've "tried" countless CRM (contact management) apps. It takes me ten seconds to log in, look around, and never think about it again. Not a huge commitment.

As always, think in terms of currency. What are they giving up to try it out? If your trial is too "cheap", you can try to increase its cost. For example, you could ask to write a case study about them after they've spent 2 weeks using it. Or you could get them to promise to try using it with their team for at least a week. If you've got a more developed product, you can take their credit card and just charge them nothing if they cancel within 30 days.

The more they are giving up for you, the more seriously you can take their validation.

"Can I buy the prototype?"

Great meeting. The best meeting conclusion I've seen is the rarely-heard but always appreciated, "Can I buy the prototype?"

A product designer was once showing me a brilliant smartphone tripod and mount he was designing. He demoed the 3D-printed prototype unit for me and I immediately asked him how much it would cost to buy it. He laughed and said he'd gone through a dozen prototypes already because people kept buying them. That's a good sign.

"When can you come back to talk to the rest of the team?"

Good meeting. Bingo! If you are selling anything to companies, you're going to have to talk to multiple people. If they won't introduce you, then it's a safe bet you're at a dead end.

Enterprise sales is tedious, but one of the perks is that you can get really accurate signals like this one quite early in the process. Building consumer products is a lot murkier since the customer conversation process doesn't mimic the purchase process as much.

HOW TO FIX A BAD MEETING

The worst meetings are the wishy-washy ones that you leave with neither rejection nor advancement. You are in no-man's-land and you won't learn anything until you fix the meeting by forcing a next step (or rejection).

A lost meeting can often be saved by just pushing for a commitment at the end while you're being brushed off with a compliment.

You don't need to be annoying or overbearing about it. You aren't trying to strong-arm folks into handing over their wallet. You're just cutting through the polite rejections to find out if they're actually on track to become a partner/investor/customer.

If they aren't excited, then good news: you got the information you came for. Assimilate it, decide if it matters enough to change your strategy, and then keep on keeping on. The goal is just to put them to a decision so you can learn whether you've found a must-have product and a real customer.

Rule of thumb: It's not a real lead until you've given them a concrete chance to reject you.

DON'T PITCH BLIND

Even once you've moved on to more product-focused sales meetings, you still want to start with some open-ended learning to get your bearings. While you may already know what the market in general cares about, figuring out this particular customer's unique situation will considerably improve the rest of the conversation. A bit of initial orientation increases your chances of closing the deal and delivers ongoing learning even after you've got a product and are in sales mode.

Startup sales meetings too often go like this:

You: "We do X. Want to buy it?"
Them: "No thanks."

This sort of rejection isn't helpful because it doesn't teach you anything. Hard pitching gives binary feedback: you either nailed it or you didn't. That's okay when you're making fine adjustments (tweak this feature) but bad for bigger questions (does anybody care at all about what I'm doing).

Ask learning questions which pass The Mom Test. Then confirm by selling it. This happens over both the life of your company and during a single meeting.

CRAZY CUSTOMERS AND YOUR FIRST SALE

It's pretty weird that anybody buys anything from young startups. In all likelihood, before the year is up, you're going to either go out of business, abandon the product, or sell the company. And even if you stay the course, there's no guarantee you can actually do what you say you can do.

First customers are crazy. Crazy in a good way. They really, really want what you're making. They want it so badly that they're willing to be the crazy person who tries it first.

Keep an eye out for the people who get emotional about what you're doing. There is a significant difference between: "Yeah, that's a problem" and "THAT IS THE WORST PART OF MY LIFE AND I WILL PAY YOU RIGHT NOW TO FIX IT."

Steve Blank calls them earlyvangelists (early evangelists). In the enterprise software world, they are the people who:

- Have the problem
- Know they have the problem
- Have the budget to solve the problem
- Have already cobbled together their own makeshift solution

They're the company who will commit way before it makes rational sense to do so. It's the guy who will give you cash right now from his discretionary budget to run a trial. Or who will fight for you against his boss and lawyers when they're saying the tech is unproven.

In the consumer space, it's the fan who wants your product to succeed so badly that they'll front you the money as a pre-order when all you've got is a duct-tape prototype. They're the one who will tell all their friends to chip in as well. They're the person reading your blog and searching for workarounds.

We've got 2 takeaways.

Firstly, when someone isn't too emotional about what you're doing, they are unlikely to end up being one of your crazy first customers. Keep them on the list and try to make them happy, of course, but don't count on them to write the first check.

Secondly, whenever you see the deep emotion, do your utmost to keep that person close. They are the rare, precious fan who will get you through the hard times and give you your first sale.

In summary: once you've learned the facts of your industry and customers and designed the solution, start pushing for advancement and commitments to separate dead leads from real customers.

Rule of thumb: In early stage sales, the real goal is learning. Revenue is a side-effect.

CHAPTER 6

FINDING CONVERSATIONS

Now that you know how to ask good questions and fix bad meetings, you know enough to have good customer conversations. Go do it! Flex your conversational muscles and talk to some people.

If you're scratching your own itch with this business, you likely already know your customers. Great! Talk to them. Now that you're armed with The Mom Test, they won't be able to lie to you even though they know you.

But if you don't already know folks, where do these conversations and meetings come from?

GOING TO THEM

Drumming up good conversations from cold leads is hard. It's doable and sometimes you have no choice, but it's far from ideal.

The goal of cold conversations is to stop having them. You hustle together the first one or two from wherever you can, and then, if you treat people's time respectfully and are genuinely trying to solve their problem, those cold conversations start turning into warm intros. The snowball is rolling.

Cold calls

What does it mean if you reach out to 100 people and 98 of them hang up on you? Well, nothing, except that people don't like getting cold calls. No surprise there. More importantly, it means you've now got 2 conversations in play. Unless your plan is to sell your app via cold calls, the rejection rate is irrelevant.

I know one team who successfully used cold LinkedIn messages to reach C-level execs of several major UK retailers. They were ignored by practically every exec in the country, but you only need one "yes" to get you started.

Beyond hard hustle, stay open to serendipity. There are lots of ways to get lucky when you're in the mood for it.

Seizing serendipity

While I was considering building tools for professional speakers, I found myself at a friend-of-a-friend's engagement party. I heard someone across the room say "...my talk in Tokyo next week" and made a beeline over to her. She left the party thinking I was a nice guy who was super interested in her career and I left with a bunch of useful customer insight. She ended up becoming my first committed alpha user.

If it sounds weird to unexpectedly interview people, then that's only because you're thinking of them as interviews instead of conversations. The only thing people love talking about more than themselves is their problems. By taking an interest in the problems and minutia of their day, you're already more interesting than 99% of the people they've ever met.

Rule of thumb: If it's not a formal meeting, you don't need to make excuses about why you're there or even mention that you're starting a business. Just ask about their life.

Find a good excuse

I was chatting to an aspiring entrepreneur in a cafe. Among other things, his product could help cafe owners educate potential customers on the origins and backstory of the coffee beans. He had been hitting the pavement for the past 2 weeks and getting turned away from cafe after cafe. He wanted to talk to me about his customer interview process. Ten minutes into the conversation, I cut in: "Who have you talked to so far?" "Nobody will take time to talk to me; they all just say to come back later." I flagged down the waitress who was walking by. "Excuse me, can I speak to the owner?" "Umm." "Don't worry, it's nothing bad. This coffee is amazing and I wanted to ask him about the story behind the beans." The owner wasn't around, but with a good excuse in hand, we were soon chatting with the manager. And the manager, in turn, gave us the owner's contact details and said he'd be in on Tuesday.

The practical downside is that no matter how well the chat goes, it's impossible to transition into a product or sales conversation, since doing so reveals your initial deception and destroys trust. When I open with an excuse, I tend to consider the chat to be a throwaway for one-time learning instead of an ongoing relationship.

You've got the ultimate excuse if you have a PhD student on your founding team. "Hello, I'm doing my PhD research on the problems around X, it would be a huge help if I could ask you a couple questions for my dissertation." If you're really desperate, you can always be "writing a book" and hoping to interview them.

Rule of thumb: If it's a topic you both care about, find an excuse to talk about it. Your idea never needs to enter the equation and you'll both enjoy the chat.

Immerse yourself in where they are

When I wanted to build tools for public speakers and conference organisers, I knew a few at the lower and middle tiers, but none of the big names who charge $5-50k per talk. Which was a problem, since I thought might be a good customer segment for obvious reasons. So I hit the conference circuit and gave free talks everywhere I could.

The speakers lounge became my personal customer conversation machine. Everywhere I went was an opportunity to meet new speakers and learn what event organisers care about. By immersing myself in the community I met a load of people and soon had all the connections and conversations I could handle (I ultimately decided that big speakers and big conferences were a bad customer segment and walked away—not every conversation has to end in finding out your idea is awesome).

Landing pages

Joel Gascoigne did a classic landing page test with his startup Buffer, describing the value proposition and collecting emails. But contrary to popular understanding, it wasn't the metrics or conversion rate which convinced him to move forward. Instead, it was the conversations which resulted from him emailing every single person who signed up and saying hello.

I'm skeptical of the quantitative value of landing page metrics. But they are certainly a great way to collect emails of qualified leads for you to reach out to and strike up a conversation with.

Paul Graham suggests that generic launch can be a solid start for the same reason. Get your product out there, see who seems to like it most, and then reach out to those types of users for deeper learning.

This is starting to bring the customers to you instead of going to them, but still involves sending a mostly cold email. Next, we'll look at how to run with this principle to make our lives even easier.

BRINGING THEM TO YOU

When you are finding ways to sneak into customer conversations, you're always on the back foot. You made the approach, so they are suspicious and trying to figure out if you're wasting their time. Instead, we should look for ways to separate ourselves from the crowd so *they* can find *us*. Beyond saving vast sums of time and frustration, bringing people to you also makes them take you more seriously and want to help you more. How can you plant a flag your customers can see? What can you offer them that will make them want to talk to you?

Organise meetups

For marginally more effort than attending an event, you can organise your own and benefit from being the centre of attention.

Want to figure out the problems HR professionals have? Organise an event called "HR professionals happy hour". People will assume you're credible just because you happen to be the person who sent the invite emails or introduced the speaker. You'll have an easy time chatting to them about their problems.

Nobody ever follows this recommendation, but it's the first

thing I would do if I moved a new industry or geography. It's the fastest and most unfair trick I've seen for rapid customer learning. As a bonus, it also bootstraps your industry credibility.

Speaking & teaching

Teaching is under-valued as both a learning and selling tool. Let's say you're making better project management software. In that case, you probably have both expertise and a strongly held opinion about how things could be better. That's the magic combination for being an effective teacher.

Spend the time to teach. You can teach at conferences, workshops, through online videos, blogging, and by doing free consulting or office hours.

You'll refine your message, get in touch with a room full of potential customers who take you seriously, and will learn which parts of your offering resonate (before you've even built it). Then simply chat up the attendees who are most keen.

Industry blogging

If you have a reasonably sized and relevant blog audience, lining up conversations is trivial. You just write a post about it and ask people to get in touch. Of course, not everyone has a relevant audience. That's one big reason to start blogging to your customers today.

Even when I had no audience, I still found blogging to be helpful. When I sent cold emails from my blog email address, folks would often meet with me because they had checked my domain, seen my industry blog, and figured I was an interesting person to talk to. In other words, the traffic and audience were irrelevant. Blogging about an industry is also a good exercise to get your thoughts in a row. It makes you a better customer conversationalist.

Get clever

I once heard a brilliant hack from a guy who wanted to sell to top-tier universities like Stanford and Harvard. But first he needed to understand their problems (difficult) and be taken seriously by the decision makers (even more difficult).

His solution was to organise a semi-monthly "knowledge exchange" call between the department heads of top universities to discuss the challenges around his topic of choice. Furthermore, it was set up as a conference call where any other universities could dial in and listen to the best practices of the big ones. By simply organising the call and playing host, he immediately absorbed all the credibility of the top universities and got direct phone access to a pile of great leads.

Every business is different. Don't just copy what someone else is doing. Consider your situation and get clever.

CREATING WARM INTROS

Warm intros are the goal. Conversations are infinitely easier when you get an intro through a mutual friend that establishes your credibility and reason for being there.

7 degrees of bacon

The world is a relatively small place. Everyone knows someone. We just have to remember to ask.

I was talking to a team of recent graduates who needed to reach McKinsey style consultants. They were pulling their hair out. We were in a co-working space full of other young entrepreneurs, so I just stood on a chair and yelled, "Excuse me, does anyone here know anyone who works at McKinsey? Can we talk to you for a second? We'll buy you a beer!" The founders bought three beers, had three quick chats, and left with a diary of intros.

This is even easier for consumer products. Not everyone knows folks at McKinsey, but everybody does know, for example, a recent mom or amateur athlete or theatre enthusiast.

Rule of thumb: Kevin Bacon's 7 degrees of separation applies to customer conversations. You can find anyone you need if you ask for it a couple times.

Industry advisors

I relied heavily on advisors in my first company. We didn't know the industry and nobody took us seriously. Our 5 advisors each had around a half percent of equity and basically just made credible intros. I met with each once per month, so I'd get a fresh batch of intros weekly without it being a huge time burden for any of them.

On a bit of a tangent, you'd be surprised by the quality of the folks you can get to join your advisory board. The first conversation with a good advisor looks similar to the first conversation with a flagship customer: you get along and are talking about a space you both care about. You can sometimes poach killer advisors from your early customer conversations.

Universities

I'm jealous of founders who are still in (or recently out of) university. Professors are a goldmine for intros. They get their grant-funding from friendly, high-level industry folks. And since they're investing in research, those industry folks are self-selected to be excited about new projects.

Professors are easy to get in touch with if you don't know them yet. They post their emails and you can generally just wander into their office.

Investors

Top-tier investors are awesome for B2B intros. Beyond their own rolodex and company portfolio, they can usually pull off cold intros to practically any industry. Investors can also help you close better advisors and directors than you'd be able to wrangle on your own.

This really applies more generally than investors to anyone who is a big deal and has already bought into your idea. Who can they connect you to?

Cash in favours

Remember all those people who brushed you off by saying, "Sounds great, keep me in the loop and let me know how I can help"?

Now's the time to call in those favours. Yes, they might not have actually meant it, but who cares? Reply back to that ancient email and tell them you're ready for an intro to that guy they know. Use the format in the next section to make their lives easy and reassure them that you aren't going to waste anybody's time.

You'll get ignored a lot, but again, who cares? You aren't trying to minimise your failure rate; you're trying to get a few conversations going. The people you're being introduced to won't know the backstory anyway, so it's a clean start from there.

I wouldn't make a habit of doing stuff like this since it's a bit annoying and can burn bridges, but sometimes you're backed into a corner and need to get started somehow.

ASKING FOR AND FRAMING THE MEETING

Sometimes a proper meeting can't be avoided. For example, you might want the full hour or need to talk to someone senior outside of your peer or networking group. But since you don't necessarily have anything to sell, it's unclear what the meeting is *for*. In those cases, the right explanation and framing can do wonders.

If you don't know why you're there, it becomes a sales meeting by default, which is bad for three reasons. First, the customer closes up about certain important topics like pricing. Second, attention shifts to you instead of them. And finally, it's going to be the worst sales meeting ever because you aren't ready.

Symptoms:

- "Um. So...."
- "How's it going?"

There are a lot of bad ways to frame the meeting, both when first asking for it and once it begins. Framing like, "Can I interview you" or "Thanks for agreeing to this interview" both set set off alarm bells that this meeting is going to be super boring. I don't want to be interviewed; I want to talk and help!

The common, "Can I get your opinion on what we're doing?" sets expectations of neediness and that you want compliments or approval.

No expectations at all are set by, "Do you have time for a

quick coffee/lunch/chat/meeting?" which suggests you're liable to waste their time.

The framing format I like has five key elements.

1. You're an entrepreneur trying to solve horrible problem X, usher in wonderful vision Y, or fix stagnant industry Z. Don't mention your idea.
2. Frame expectations by mentioning what stage you're at and, if it's true, that you don't have anything to sell.
3. Show weakness and give them a chance to help by mentioning the specific problem that you're looking for answers on. This will also clarify that you're not a time waster.
4. Put them on a pedestal by showing how much they, in particular, can help.
5. Explicitly ask for help.

Or, in shorter form: **Vision / Framing / Weakness / Pedestal / Ask**

The mnemonic is "Very Few Wizards Properly Ask [for help]." Here's what it might look like before you have a product:

> Hey Pete,
>
> I'm trying to make desk & office rental less of a pain for new businesses (*vision*). We're just starting out and don't have anything to sell, but want to make sure we're building something that actually helps (*framing*).
>
> I've only ever come at it from the tenant's side and I'm having a hard time understanding how it all works from

> the landlord's perspective (*weakness*). You've been renting out desks for a while and could really help me cut through the fog (*pedestal*).
>
> Do you have time in the next couple weeks to meet up for a chat? (*ask*)

Sometimes the 5 parts will be combined into just one or two sentences, or they can be in a different order. For example, when I originally wrote it, the next email sounded a little too pitchy and I was worried he would delete it as sales spam. As such, I moved my admission of weakness as early as I could get it:

> Hey Scott, I run a startup trying to make advertising more playful and ultimately effective (*vision*).
>
> We're having a load of trouble figuring out how all the pieces of the industry fit together and where we can best fit into it (*weakness*). You know more about this industry than anyone and could really save us from a ton of mistakes (*pedestal*).
>
> We're funded and have a couple products out already, but this is in no way a sales meeting -- we're just moving into a new area and could really use some of your expertise (*framing*).
>
> Can you spare a bit of time in the next week to help point us in the right direction over a coffee? (*ask*)

People like to help entrepreneurs. But they also hate wasting their time. An opening like this tells them that you know what you need and that they'll be able to make a real difference.

Once the meeting starts, you have to grab the reins or it's liable to turn into them drilling you on your idea, which is exactly what you don't want (since that forces you into a pitching situation, thus destroying your learning).

To set the meeting framing and agenda, I basically repeat what I said in the email and then immediately drop into the first question. If someone else made the introduction, use them as a voice of authority:

> Hey Tim, thanks so much for taking the time.
>
> As I mentioned in the email, we're trying to make it easier for universities to spin out student businesses (*vision*) and aren't exactly sure how it all works yet (*framing & weakness*).
>
> Tom (*authority*) connected us because you have pretty unique insight into what's going on behind the curtain and could really help us get pointed in the right direction (*pedestal*)... (*introductions continue*)
>
> I was looking at your spinout portfolio and it's pretty impressive, especially company X. How did they get from your classroom to where they are now? (*grab the reins and ask good questions*)

These conversations are easy to screw up. As such, you need to be the one in control. You set the agenda, you keep it on topic, and you propose next steps. Don't be a jerk about it, but do have a plan for the meeting and be assertive about keeping it on track.

Once again, you can only pull this off if you have prepared your list of 3 big learning goals and have an idea of some possible next steps and commitments that you can ask for if the meeting goes well.

It's worth noting that this is how I set up meetings from warm intros. Warm intros mean the person wants to give you the benefit of the doubt, but is still terrified you're going to waste their time with a vague, chit-chatty meeting. The goal with this the VFWPA structure is to specify exactly what I need and how they, in particular can help. This answers their biggest fear in accepting the meeting and you'll see really high response rates.

Cold approaches are a different beast and I haven't found a magic bullet or reliable cold email format. But remember, the point of cold calls is to stop having them. If you're banging your head against the wall trying to get people to answer your cold emails, then you're probably taking the hard road. Spend your energy finding clever ways to generate warm intros instead. You'll have a much easier time.

TO COMMUTE OR TO CALL

One of the solutions to the time cost of these conversations is to move them onto Skype or phone calls. In most situations, I don't think the added volume is worth the information you lose by not being in the room. I get confused enough by what people are telling me in person. Losing access to their face and body language feels like shooting myself in the foot.

More subtly, calls damage the delicate power dynamic of these conversations. When someone is having a coffee with you, there's the potential to chat as friends. You can just shoot the breeze about the industry for a bit. You can keep it casual. They're enjoying the conversation.

The same is decidedly not true on the phone or Skype. People try to squeeze calls in between other activities, wondering how quickly they can "finish with business" and hang up. Folks on the phone are super annoyed when you "just want to chat". So you need to make the whole thing more formal, which is one of the exact mistakes we're trying to avoid!

Phone calls end up sounding more like scripted interviews than natural conversations, because they are. It's a constraint of the medium.

Plus, nobody becomes friends over the phone, which means you aren't going to get the warm intros and future meetings you need. Setting up a call feels faster in the short-term, but that's because you aren't yet able to see all the time-saving and business-saving benefits of in-person relationships with your customers.

That being said, some other great people in the field like and recommend phone calls. Use whatever works. But I will say that you should *start* in person. It's too easy to use surveys or phone calls as an excuse to skip the awkwardness of meeting in person rather than as a considered trade-off.

THE ADVISORY FLIP

In terms of mindset, don't go into these discussions looking for customers. It creates a needy vibe and forfeits the position of power. Instead, go in search of industry and customer advisors. You are just trying to find helpful, knowledgable people who are excited about your idea.

With that mindset switch, you'll know why you're there. And instead of it being a customer-learning-but-I-really-want-to-do-sales meeting, it becomes a let-me-find-out-if-you-are-a-good-advisor-by-asking-questions meeting.

Willpower is a finite resource. The way to overcome difficult situations isn't to power through, but rather to change your circumstances to require less willpower. Changing the context of the meeting to "looking for advisors" is the equivalent of throwing out all your chocolate when you start a diet. You change the environment to naturally facilitate your goals.

You don't need to explicitly tell them you're looking for advisors. In fact, I wouldn't unless you already quite like them and it happens to come up in conversation. It's really about orienting your state of mind to give you a helpful internal narrative and consistent front.

Somewhat counterintuitively, the sales-advisor switch also puts you firmly in control of the meeting, since you're now evaluating *them*. Even if the topics of discussion are basically the same, you (and they) will notice the difference.

HOW MANY MEETINGS

Every meeting has an opportunity cost. When you're traveling to that meeting, you aren't writing code or generating leads or drinking margaritas.

If you're running a sales-driven business (especially enterprise sales), the opportunity cost of early conversations is low since many of them will become sales leads. You're doubling up on learning and dealflow.

The UX community (who knows their customer conversation!) says you should keep talking to people until you stop hearing new information.

Under perfect circumstances where your first guesses are mostly correct and you're in a relatively simple industry that you already understand, then you it might only take 3-5 conversations to confirm what you already believe. But you usually won't get so lucky, and it will take quite a few more until you start hearing a consistent message from the folks you're talking to. If you've run more than 10 conversations and are still getting results that are all over the map, then it's possible that your customer segment is too vague, which means you're mashing together feedback from multiple different types of customers.

It's not about "how many" meetings. It's about having enough for you to really understand your customers. You want to talk to them enough that know them in the same way you know your close friends, with a firm grip on their goals, their frustrations, what else they've tried, and how they currently deal with it.

This isn't about having a thousand meetings. It's about quickly learning what you need, and then getting back to building your business. The overall process of learning is never finished, but in most cases you should be able to answer almost any individual question about your business or your customers (and then move onto new ones) within a week.

Rule of thumb: Keep having conversations until you stop hearing new stuff.

CHAPTER 7

CHOOSING YOUR CUSTOMERS

They say that startups don't starve, they drown. You never have too few options, too few leads, or too few ideas; you have too many. You get overwhelmed. You do a little bit of everything. When it comes to getting above water and making faster progress, good customer segmentation is your best friend.

SEGMENTATION

When we look at the big successes, they seem to serve the whole world. Google lets anyone find anything. Paypal helps anyone send money anywhere. Evernote backs up all the writing of everybody.

But they didn't start there. If you start too generic, everything is watered down. Your marketing message is generic. You suffer feature creep. In their early days, Google helped PhD students find obscure bits of code. Paypal helped collectors buy and sell Pez dispensers and Beanie Babies more efficiently. Evernote helped moms save and share recipes.

When you have a fuzzy sense of who you're serving, you end

up talking to a multiple customer segments all at once, which leads to confusing signals and three problems:

1. You get overwhelmed by options and don't know where to start
2. You aren't moving forward but can't prove yourself wrong
3. You receive mixed feedback and can't make sense of it

Babies or body builders?

I talked to a woman who had developed a very cool powdered condiment. It was sweet (like a cinnamon brown sugar), but had all the nutrition of a multivitamin. In fact, it was an all-natural superfood: you survive indefinitely eating nothing but that powder.

She said it had countless uses: you could sprinkle it on your breakfast or mix it in with your protein shake. Moms could trick their kids into being healthy. Restaurants could leave it on the tables as a healthy sugar alternative. However, she was running in circles because the bodybuilders wanted one thing, the restaurants wanted another, and the moms needed a third. Making one of them happy always disappointed the others. She didn't know how to start. Even simple problems like which colour to use for the label were impossible to answer.

Before we can serve *everyone*, we have to serve *someone*. Forgetting about all the possibilities and focusing on who would *most likely* buy, she decided it was moms with young kids who are currently shopping at health food stores. She also knew where to find them: in the health food stores! But the stores were an important partner and she didn't know what they would want.

She found a way to kill two birds with one stone by going into only the small, independent health food stores and asking them to place a few bottles of her condiment beside the breakfast foods. It's a great commitment to ask for (some shelf space) that would help distinguish between kind words and serious retailers. She would return in a week to ask them about their experiences. If the stores were happy and the product sold, she could begin finding ways to talk to their customers (and her end consumers), perhaps via an in-store tasting.

This journey sounds obvious when we look at it as a case study. But when we're in the moment, choosing a really specific customer segment just feels like we're losing all the other options. And that loss is painful. Remind yourself that you'll get to the whole world eventually. But you've got to start somewhere specific.

Big brands or mom & pop?

I was once thrilled that my customer segment was "advertisers". Everyone advertises somehow, so naturally this was very exciting. Our market was practically infinite! I talked to mom-and-pop shops, e-tailers, big brands, creative agencies, SMEs, music labels and more. Everyone I talked to had different needs, constraints, problems, and desires.

Everything we tried ended up *sort of* working. Everything was *somewhat* promising. Some people were talking about paying us $10,000/month while others scoffed at the idea of paying $10. Every new feature was moderately popular. But if we tried to cut any of those middling features, we would get an uproar. It was always someone's favourite part.

In reality, our customer segment was just too broad. We were trying to serve everyone simultaneously. We said "yes" to every request. Every debate over a new feature could be won by claiming, "Well, *those* guys would love it." The reverse argument could be made to prevent any feature's removal.

The big trouble was that we could prove ourselves neither right nor wrong. We could never say that a new idea had really worked or totally failed. We were paying attention to so many customer segments that there was pretty much always someone it worked for. But making a so-so product for a bunch of audiences isn't quite the same as making an incredible product for one.

Getting specific about your ideal customers allows you to filter out all the noise which comes from everyone else. In our case, we eventually noticed unusually strong signals from creative agencies who wanted to be edgy. We ignored everyone who wasn't them, cut a bunch of features and were finally able to get a sense of what was working and what wasn't.

But what does it mean!?

I recently spoke to a couple founders who have been working hard on their customer conversations. They were using every sales meeting as an opportunity to learn. They were asking good questions which pass The Mom Test and were pushing for advancement and commitment whenever it was relevant. And yet, they were still super confused and weren't sure how to move the business to the next level. They couldn't decide which features to build and which to cut. They didn't know how to improve their marketing language. To make matters worse, the feedback they were getting was wildly inconsistent. If they ran twenty conversations, they ended up with twenty different must-have features and twenty separate must-solve problems. The more people they talked to, the more confused they got. What was going on here?

Their customer segment was incredibly broad, but in a sneaky way. Imagine that we're building something for "students". I've got a picture of an American undergraduate in my head, and maybe you picture a British grad student, but we manage to agree on features and start building.

Once we launch, the feedback starts coming in. But it's not what we expect. One user needs to add formal citations. Another wants practice questions. A third needs it to run on the iPad. A fourth needs eighty collaborators who can share the same computer. The next needs to use the app through an intermittent internet connection. We're looking at this list of requirements and our soul feels like it's being forced through a colander. This will literally take us years to build. Where do we start?

It turns out that "students" is a broader segment than we initially expected. The first is a PhD student. The second is an ambitious youngling at a prep school. The third is a home-schooling parent who wants to use it with her kid. The fourth is a rural village in the Indian rice belt where the local kids are self-educating through the one shared computer. The fifth is in Africa, running the app off a shaky cellphone connection. All are "students".

The confused founders we met at the beginning of this section were having the same experience, but for "sales organisations" instead of "students". There are countless kinds of sales organisations with fundamentally different needs, workflows, tools and goals. But from the outside, they all look like companies who do sales. Even if you narrow it down with a demographic constraint, as these guys did (sales organisations with 25-250 salespeople), you're still facing impossible amounts of variation.

These guys weren't having 20 conversations with their customers. They were having one conversation each with 20 different types of customers. That's why the feedback was so inconsistent.

In these cases, an industry expert can be hugely helpful in providing a taxonomy of the industry. It will give you a better starting point for choosing where to begin. If you don't have access to this high-level view, you still want to take your best guess and get specific. The next section on Customer Slicing is one way to approach it. Over time, your understanding of the industry will improve and you can adjust your mental categories as needed. When your customer feedback is all over the map, you can't extract value. Once you get specific, you can learn.

Rule of thumb: If you aren't finding consistent problems and goals, you don't have a specific enough customer segment.

CUSTOMER SLICING

If you're facing a generic or varied set of customer segments, you can use Customer Slicing to pick a concrete starting point. Start with any segment and then keep slicing off better and better subsets of it until you've got a tangible sense of who you can go talk to and where you can find them. Start with a broad segment and ask:

- Within this group, which type of person would want it most?
- Would everyone within this group buy/use it, or only some?
- Why does that sub-set want it? (e.g. what is their specific problem)
- Does everyone in the group have that motivation or only some?
- What additional motivations are there?
- Which other types of people have these motivations?

You'll have two sets of answers: the first is a collection of demographic groups and the second is a set of goals/motivations. Some will still be fairly generic. Go back through the generic ones and keep slicing. Just repeat the questions above. Within that sub-group, who wants it most? Repeat, repeat.

As a quick example, say I'm building some sort of high-end fitness gadget for busy professionals. It's going to be expensive, so I figure they have to be high-income (finance professionals?), and it's going to be digital, so I imagine they'll be young (25-35?). And finance professionals live in big cities, so we'll tack that on.

So my customer segment is "finance professionals, age 25-35, living in a major city", right? No! This is a totally worthless segment because it doesn't help me make better decisions and doesn't help me find them.

On the other hand, if I slice it down further to the sub-group who wants it most, then I can get somewhere. We could slice that initial segment into something like: finance professionals in London currently training for a marathon. Better! We know this slice is taking fitness seriously, so we might suspect they're stronger early adopters. We could slice that even further by saying that we want the sub-sub-subset who go to the gym during their lunch hour. Now we can have all the customer conversations we desire for the price of a membership to a gym in London's financial district.

If there isn't a clear physical or digital location at which you can find your customer segment, then it's probably still too broad. Go back up the list and slice it into finer pieces until you know where to find them. A customer segment isn't very useful if there's no way you can get in touch.

Now that we have a bunch of who-where pairs, we can decide who to start with based on who seems most:

1. Profitable or big
2. Easy to reach

3. Personally rewarding

Don't plan and theorise forever about this stuff. Just spend a few minutes to reach to a concrete initial segment so you can go find a few of them and move the business forward.

As we mentioned, you'll broaden your segment back out later. But your learning will go faster (and be more useful) for now by choosing someone who is specific and who also and meets the three big criteria of being reachable, profitable, and personally rewarding.

On a personal note, I really feel that third factor is important; it's worth choosing customers you admire and enjoy being around. This stuff is hard work and can be a real grind if you're cynical about the people or the industry you're trying to understand and serve.

Rule of thumb: Good customer segments are a who-where pair. If you don't know where to go to find your customers, keep slicing your segment into smaller pieces until you do.

TALKING TO THE WRONG PEOPLE

You can't get the data you need if you're talking to the wrong people. There are 3 ways to end up fall into this clearly unhelpful trap.

1. You have too-broad of a segment and are talking to everyone
2. You have multiple customer segments and missed some of them
3. You are selling to businesses with a complicated

buying process and have overlooked some of the stakeholders

We've already talked about #1. If you talk to everyone, many of them are inevitably going to be wrong.

Regarding #2 and 3, you can miss segments and overlook buyers in lots of ways. The first important step is to know they exist. Sometimes it's obvious. If you are a multi-sided marketplace, you clearly have multiple customer segments.

Other times it's sneakier. If you're building an app for kids, you need to understand and sell to both them and their parents. If you're building something for public schools, you need to understand the teachers, the students, the administration, and potentially even the parent-teacher association and the tax payers.

You'll also need to worry about multiple groups if you rely on an important partner, whether for manufacturing, distribution, or promotion. If your business relies on them, you'd better understand their goals and constraints just as well as you understand those of your customers.

Don't fall into the trap of only talking to the most senior or important people you can find. You want to talk to people who are representative of your customers, not the ones who sound impressive on your status report. When I was building interactive advertising products, I spent lots of time talking to executives and none talking to the kids who were supposed to love our products.

A common question is whether you need to run customer conversations separately for all the various segments in a multi-sided marketplace. Yes, you do. But hopefully that isn't quite so scary now that you know how to Keep it Casual and reduce the time cost of your learning.

CHAPTER 8

RUNNING THE PROCESS

Even if you do everything else right, you can get bad results without the right process wrapped around your conversations. Showing up and hoping for the best isn't making a good use of anyone's time. You need to do a little bit of work before and after to extract full value.

A common anti-pattern is for the business guy to go to all the meetings and subsequently tell the rest of the team what they should do. Bad idea. Telling the rest of the team "What I learned" is functionally equivalent to telling them "What you'll do." Therefore, owning the customer conversations creates a de-facto dictator with "The customer said so" as the ultimate trump card.

And that's a problem because, as we've seen, it's easy to misinterpret what the customer said.

When all the customer learning is stuck in someone's head instead of being disseminated to the rest of the team, you've got a learning bottleneck. Avoid creating (or being) the bottleneck. To do that, the learning must be shared with the entire founding team promptly and faithfully, which depends on good notes plus a bit of pre- and post-meeting work.

The most extreme way to bottleneck is to go to the meetings alone and take crappy notes which you don't review with your team. At that point, your head has become the ultimate repository of customer truth and everyone just has to do what you say.

In my case, I once bottlenecked so hard that our CTO quit while saying, "We're never going to succeed if you keep changing what we're doing." In my defence, the stuff I'd learned was true (at least, I think it was). But it didn't matter anyway since I hadn't properly communicated it to the rest of the team.

Learning bottlenecks can be created from either end: the founder in touch with customers can do a bad job of sharing it, or the product team can refuse to engage with customers and what they say.

Symptoms of a learning bottleneck:

- "You just worry about the product. I'll handle the customers."
- "Because the customers told me so!"
- "I don't have time to talk to people — I need to be coding!"

Avoiding bottlenecks has three parts: prepping, reviewing, and taking good notes.

PREPPING

Your most important preparation work is to ensure you know your current list of 3 big questions. Figure them out with your team and make a point to face the scary questions.

If you've already learned the facts of your customer and industry, then you should also know what commitment and next steps you are going to push for at the end of the meeting.

It's easier to guide the conversation and stay on track if you have an existing set of beliefs that you're updating. Spend up to an hour writing down your best guesses about what the person you're about to talk to cares about and wants. You'll probably be wrong, but it's easier to keep the discussion on track and hit important points if you've created a skeleton. If you have an appropriately focused segment, then you'll only rarely need to do this.

While prepping, if you come across a question which could be answered with desk research, take a moment to do it. You want to move past the obvious stuff and use your in-person conversations to find insights the internet can't give you.

Similarly, if you're about to meet with a business, do your basic due diligence on LinkedIn and the company website. It takes 5 minutes and will save you from trashing the conversation and looking like an idiot.

Sit down with your whole founding team when you prep. You want both business and product to be represented. If you leave part of the company out of the prep, then you end up missing their concerns in the customer conversations.

Some founders react with hostility to the whole idea. They'll say something along the lines of, "We just need to be building the darn product, not wasting our time talking to people!" This is a reasonable reaction if they feel like the customer conversations are a waste of time. And that could actually be the case if you've been doing them wrong.

The minimum prep is to ask a grumpy cofounder to "humour me" and then spend ten minutes picking the right learning goals for the upcoming conversations. Once you start having conversations that save time instead of costing it, everyone will come around.

These aren't long, involved strategy discussions. Your gut reaction is enough. You don't need to be so rigorous. A little prep goes a long way, but you do need a little. All you're really trying to figure out is:

- What do we want to learn from these guys?

Rule of thumb: If you don't know what you're trying to learn, you shouldn't bother having the conversation.

REVIEWING

After a conversation, just review your notes with your team and update your beliefs and big three questions as appropriate.

The goal is to ensure the learning is now on paper and in everyone's head instead of just in yours. Talk through the key quotes and main takeaways of the conversation, as well as any problems you ran into.

I also like to talk about the meta-level of the conversation itself: which questions worked and which didn't? How can we do better next time? Were there any important signals or questions we missed? This stuff is more craft than science: you have to actively practice it to get better. It's a valuable skill for your team to have, so it's worth spending a bit of time improving.

Just like prepping, reviewing is so simple that it sounds like a non-step. It's tempting to skip it. Don't! The review is important. Disseminate learnings to your team as quickly and as directly as possible, using notes and exact quotes wherever you can. It keeps you in sync, leads to better decisions, prevents arguments, and allows your whole team to benefit from the learning you've worked so hard to acquire.

On a logistical level, some teams have a quick chat about the results of each meeting as soon as they get back to the office. Others have longer weekly meetings to go through all the week's notes and learnings. To deal with working remotely at Founder-Centric, we keep a chat window open exclusively for sharing our customer learnings whenever we finish a meeting.

WHO SHOULD SHOW UP

Everyone on the team who is making big decisions (including tech decisions) needs to be involved in at least the occasional customer conversation. The tech guys don't need to be at most of them, but you'll all learn a ton from hearing customer reactions first-hand. You'll also be able to help each other catch and fix your conversation mistakes and biases.

Meetings go best when you've got two people at them. One person can focus on taking notes and the other can focus on talking. As the second person, you may notice the lead asking bad questions or missing a signal they should be digging into. Just jump in and fix them.

Don't send more than two people unless it's group-on-group or you've got a particularly good reason to do so. Three folks interviewing someone can be a little overwhelming.

Going in solo is fine once you get good at taking concise notes. The main problem of running solo is that it's harder to catch yourself when you start going off-track by pitching, asking bad questions, or missing the point.

If you're shy and have no cofounder to take the lead, call in a favour with a friend to come to your first couple conversations with you. Play the more passive role of the note-taker until you're comfortable. If there's no workaround and you have to bite the bullet, remember that confidence is domain-specific and that it will stop being so awkward as you do it more. Focus on understanding the process and getting better.

You can't outsource or hire someone to do customer learning. There are exceptional team dynamics where it works, but generally speaking, the founders need to be in the meetings themselves. When a hired gun brings you bad news ("The problem isn't real and nobody cares"), properly assimilating it is difficult.

More insidiously, if the signal is lukewarm, it's tempting for a hire to gloss over it. Hiring out your learning is a guaranteed way to get bad signals. Until you've got a working business model and a repeatable sales or marketing process, the founders need to be in the meetings themselves.

On the bright side, even though you have to be in the room to process the learning, you don't necessarily have to be the one setting up or leading the meetings. You can hire people to help as long as you're there with them, listening.

HOW TO WRITE IT DOWN

Taking good notes is the best way to keep your team (and investors and advisors) in the loop. Plus, notes make it harder to lie to yourself. And when, months later, you decide to adjust the business's direction, you'll be able to return to your notes instead of having to go do a whole new set of interviews.

When possible, write down exact quotes. Wrap them in quotation marks so you know it's verbatim. You can later use them in your marketing language, fundraising decks, and to resolve arguments with skeptical teammates. Other times the details aren't so relevant and you can just jot down the gist.

In either case, add symbols to your notes as context and shorthand. I use about a dozen main symbols and make up more in the field as needed. You probably won't exactly copy mine, so don't worry about memorising them. You'll build your own go-to list as you have more conversations.

:) :(:| ⚡ ⊓ ☐ ⤴ ^ ☑ $ ♀ ☆

Emotions

:) Excited
:(Angry
:| Embarrassed

Someone saying "that's a problem" can be interpreted totally differently depending on whether they are neutral or outraged. Any strong emotion is worth writing down. For example, depending on your industry, you might also choose to make symbols for lust, envy or laughter. Capture the big emotions and remember to dig into them when they come up.

Their life

⚡ Pain or problem (symbol is a lightning bolt)
⊓ Goal or job-to-be-done (symbol is a soccer/football goal)
☐ Obstacle
⤴ Workaround
^ Background or context (symbol is a distant mountain)

These five "life" symbols are your bread and butter. Combine them with emotion symbols where appropriate. Pains and obstacles carry a lot more weight when someone is embarrassed or angry about them.

Obstacles are preventing a customer from solving their problems even though they want to. They're important because you'll probably also have to deal with them. For example, a lot of corporate folks would *love* to use cloud services and *hate* their current tools, but can't, because their company's IT policy is an obstacle. Their workaround might be to use their personal phone as a secondary computer or by doing certain work at home. Also worth noting.

Specifics

☑ Feature request or purchasing criteria
$ Money or budgets or purchasing process
♀ Mentioned a specific person or company
☆ Follow-up task

As we discussed, feature requests usually get ignored, but they're a good signal to capture and explore. Must-have purchasing criteria are obviously more important. Money signals are also key.

Write down specific names and companies. If it's someone they know, ask for an intro at the end of the conversation. If it's a competitor or alternate solution, write it down to research it later.

Put a big star on items to follow-up on after the meeting, especially next-steps you promised as a condition of their advancement/commitment.

WHERE TO WRITE IT DOWN

You want to take your customer notes so that they are:

- Able to be sorted, mixed, and re-arranged

- Able to be combined with the notes of the rest of your team
- Permanent and retrievable
- Not mixed in with other random noise like todo lists and ideas

In practice, I've found that taking notes in my primary notebook is practically useless. Over the course of several months' sprawl, you set an insurmountable search and retrieval task for yourself. If you won't look at your notes, they aren't much good.

If you do end up taking notes in non-ideal places, you just need to spend a little extra post-meeting time moving them over into your permanent format. Otherwise you'll be kicking yourself when you don't entirely remember that amazing quote you'd love to put on your website.

What is a better note-taking medium?

Google Docs spreadsheets and Evernote are both great for team sharing, search, and retrieval. Spreadsheets are wonderfully sortable if you write your key signals in their own column. The downside is that it comes across as rude to take notes directly on a computer during a meeting, so you add a bit of mandatory post-meeting work to transfer your notes. I always found this a bit annoying, but it's way better than losing your learning in an off-topic notebook.

A dedicated notebook is fine, if you can remember to carry it with you and use it. For a while, I would use my regular notebook for my customer notes and then just tear out every page which wasn't from an interview so it was easier to find them later. Hardly the most elegant.

My favourite medium is index cards. Post-it notes also work. I carry around blank cards and take notes on them, with one quote or learning per card (along with a signal icon, of course). After the meeting I jot down the date and who I was talking to. If your whole team uses cards for their conversations, you can lay them all out on the table for easy access and sorting. For example, if you learn that the you're solving a non-problem, you can just pull out all the cards marked with a lightning bolt and find yourself a new problem that customers have already validated for you.

When I first started, I would make audio recordings, but that suffered from the same problem as notebooks: I'd end up with a ton of content and no real way to sort it or find the bit I wanted. If you *do* want to use audio, you'll find people are surprisingly willing to be recorded. Put your phone on the table as you sit down and say, "Hey, is it cool if I record this, because I'm always paranoid I'll miss something important in my notes. It won't get shared with anyone or posted anywhere." Almost everyone says yes, but it does blow your cover if you're trying to Keep it Casual.

If you embrace Keeping it Casual, you'll find customer conversations appearing out of nowhere and catching you by surprise. Just go with it. I've got notes written on paper plates from a pizza party, on beer mats from the pub, and on newspapers from the cafe. Just transfer them over to your main storage system once you get back to the office. It's better to capture what's said on something weird than to try to remember all the important bits.

If it's totally inappropriate to take notes during the chat, just have the conversation and then immediately retreat to a corner to write down what was said. This is how I usually handle customer conversations at the pub or conferences.

Regardless of the medium, the most important thing is that the notes are lightweight enough that you'll actually review them yourself and with your team.

Rule of thumb: Notes are useless if you don't look at them.

THE PROCESS

Talking to customers is a tool, not an obligation. If it's not going to help or you don't want to do it for whatever reason, just skip it. I'm sure you've been on the receiving end of a half-assed survey sent out by some new startup to tick the box marked "learn from customers" on their startup todo list. There are better ways to waste your time.

Without figuring out what actually matters to your company and how to deal with it effectively, you're just going through the motions.

Warning signs that you're just going through the motions:

- You're talking more than they are
- They are complimenting you or your idea
- You told them about your idea and don't have next steps
- You don't have notes
- You haven't looked through your notes with your team
- You got an unexpected answer and it didn't change your idea
- You weren't scared of any of the questions you asked
- You aren't sure what you're trying to learn in this conversation

The persistent presence of any of these problems suggests that you're doing something wrong and wasting your time.

Here are the steps I go through to keep on track. Feel free to ignore or tweak as needed given your situation and company. It's as light-weight as I've been able to get it and should reduce rather than increase the amount of time you need to spend on conversations.

The process before a batch of conversations:

- If you haven't yet, choose a focused, findable segment
- With your team, decide your big 3 learning goals
- If relevant, decide on ideal next steps and commitments
- If conversations are the right tool, figure out who to talk to
- Create a series of best guesses about what the person cares about
- If a question could be answered via desk research, do that first

During the conversation:

- Frame the conversation
- Keep it casual
- Ask good questions which pass The Mom Test
- Deflect compliments, anchor fluff, and dig beneath signals
- Take good notes
- If relevant, press for commitment and next steps

After a batch of conversations:

- With your team, review your notes and key customer quotes
- If relevant, transfer notes into permanent storage
- Update your beliefs and plans
- Decide on the next 3 big questions

The goal of this process is twofold. First, to ensure you're spending your time well by attacking the questions which really matter and making use of the brains of the whole founding team. Second, to spread any new learning through your team as quickly and completely as possible.

There you go. Now you know everything I do about how to learn from conversations. Combine this process with The Mom Test, Keeping it Casual, and Advancement for maximum learning in minimum time. But even if it goes wrong, don't worry so much. Eternity will forgive.

THIS STUFF IS FAST

The time scales of the process are important. The point is to make your business move faster, not slower.

Don't spend a week prepping for meetings; spend an hour and then go talk to people. Anything more is stalling.

Don't spend months doing full-time customer conversations before beginning to move on a product. Spend a week, maybe two. Get your bearings and then give them something to commit to.

You'll keep talking to customers for the life of your company, of course. I'm not advising you to become a recluse after the first two weeks. Your customers are a crucial source of ongoing insight. With the tools in this book (especially Keeping it Casual) you should be able to keep benefitting from customer learning without feeling like you're wasting so much time on it. You can do it alongside growing your business rather than in place of it.

Customer learning can move really quickly when you're doing it right. This book isn't meant to give you an excuse to squander precious months theorising and planning the "perfect question". It's meant to help you extract maximum value in minimum time so you can get back to what really matters: building your business.

Rule of thumb: Go build your dang company already.

CONCLUSION AND CHEATSHEET

I still ask dumb questions all the time. You will too. Don't beat yourself up over it. In fact, just yesterday I screwed up a particularly important meeting by slipping into pitch mode (this was yesterday at the time of writing... hopefully not again at the time of reading).

It happens. It's okay. Review with your team, don't beat yourself up (or your cofounders) over mistakes. Work on getting better as a team.

I make tons of mistakes. At least now I notice and have a chance to fix them. Most bad conversations can be fixed. You're trying to do something difficult. You're never going to be perfect, but it always helps to be better.

People love startups. Startups do cool stuff and make their lives better. When entrepreneurs screw up, people want to forgive them. They want the entrepreneur and the startup to succeed.

By asking good questions, we can fix many flawed ideas before they get us in trouble. But still, sometimes it doesn't work out. It's okay. Go to the people who supported you and thank them. They'll say something like:

"Hey, don't even worry about it — I know how it goes."

Rule of thumb: It's going to be okay.

HACK IT

In ancient times it was prophesied that whoever undid the convoluted Gordian Knot would rule the land. Coming across the knot, Alexander drew his sword and with a single stroke, cut it in half. The knot was undone and he became "the Great".

Struggling to untie the knot was the "proper" process. Cutting through it was a hack (ba-dum tish!) which got Alexander straight to the end result without any of the work.

When we find a new and exciting process, it's easy to do the opposite and spend hours obsessively geeking out about exactly the right way to untie this big, gnarly knot.

I remember being at a workshop about customer segmentation, a personal trainer said he was spending most of his time on the non-billable commute between his clients. At some point it was suggested that the police might be a better customer, since he could go to the station and spend all day working with different officers. No commute, more billable hours, and a less price-sensitive customer. Sounds good in theory!

We all started geeking out about how he was going to validate this. Who could he talk to? Did anyone have family in the police? What should his interview questions be? What was the market size? Etc etc.

He looked at us like we were all idiots and held up his phone.

"Actually, I think I'll just call them." It's not like he didn't know their number. We all stood around a bit dumbfounded while he went outside and called the police. Twenty minutes later, he came back in with a trial session scheduled.

Having a process is valuable, but don't get stuck in it. Sometimes you can just pick up the phone and hack through the knot.

CHEATSHEET

Just in case you like lists.

Key skills:

- Asking good questions (Chapters 1 & 3)
- Avoiding bad data (Chapter 2)
- Keeping it casual (Chapter 4)
- Pushing for commitment & advancement (Chapter 5)
- Framing the meeting (Chapter 6)
- Customer segmentation (Chapter 7)
- Prepping & reviewing (Chapter 8)
- Taking notes (Chapter 8)

The Mom Test:

1. Talk about their life instead of your idea
2. Ask about specifics in the past instead of generics or opinions about the future
3. Talk less and listen more

Getting back on track (avoiding bad data):

- Deflect compliments
- Anchor fluff
- Dig beneath opinions, ideas, requests, and emotions

Mistakes and symptoms:

1. Fishing for compliments. "I'm thinking of starting a business... so, do you think it will work?" "I had an awesome idea for an app — do you like it?"
2. Exposing your ego (aka The Pathos Problem). "So here's that top-secret project I quit my job for... what do you think?" "I can take it — be honest and tell me what you really think!"
3. Being pitchy. "No no, I don't think you get it..." "Yes, but it also does this!"
4. Being too formal. "So, first off, thanks for agreeing to this interview. I just have a few questions for you and then I'll let you get back to your day..." "On a scale of 1 to 5, how much would you say you..." "Let's set up a meeting."
5. Being a learning bottleneck. "You just worry about the product. I'll handle the customers." "Because the customers told me so!" "I don't have time to talk to people — I need to get back to coding!"
6. Collecting compliments instead of facts and commitments. "We're getting a lot of positive feedback." "Everybody I've talked to loves the idea."

The process before, during and after the meeting:

- If you haven't yet, choose a focused, findable segment

- With your team, decide your big 3 learning goals
- If relevant, decide on ideal next steps and commitments
- If conversations are the right tool, figure out who to talk to
- Create a series of your best guesses about what the person cares about
- If a question could be answered via desk research, do that first

- Frame the conversation
- Keep it casual
- Ask good questions which pass The Mom Test
- Deflect compliments, anchor fluff, and dig beneath signals
- Take good notes
- If relevant, press for commitment and next steps

- With your team, review your notes and key customer quotes
- If relevant, transfer notes into permanent storage
- Update your beliefs and plans
- Decide on the next 3 big questions

Results of a good meeting:

- Facts — concrete, specific facts about what they do

and why they do it (as opposed to the bad data of compliments, fluff, and opinions)
- Commitment — They are showing they're serious by giving up something they value such as meaningful amounts of time, reputation risk, or money
- Advancement — They are moving to the next step of your real-world funnel and getting closer to a sale

Signs you're just going through the motions:

- You're talking more than they are
- They are complimenting you or your idea
- You told them about your idea and don't have next steps
- You don't have notes
- You haven't looked through your notes with your team
- You got an unexpected answer and it didn't change your idea
- You weren't scared of any of the questions you asked
- You aren't sure which big question you're trying to answer
- You aren't sure why you're having the meeting

Writing it down — signal symbols:

:)Excited
:(Angry
:|Embarrassed
‹ Pain or problem (symbol is a lightning bolt)
⊓ Goal or job-to-be-done (symbol is a soccer/football goal)
□ Obstacle

⤴Workaround
^Background or context (symbol is a distant mountain)
☑ Feature request or purchasing criteria
$ Money or budgets or purchasing process
♀ Mentioned a specific person or company
☆ Follow-up task

Signs you aren't pushing for commitment and advancement:

- A pipeline of zombie leads
- Ending product meetings with a compliment
- Ending product meetings with no clear next steps
- Meetings which "went well"
- They haven't given up anything of value

Asking for and framing the meeting:

- Vision — half-sentence of how you're making the world better
- Framing — where you're at and what you're looking for
- Weakness — where you're stuck and how you can be helped
- Pedestal — show that they, in particular, can provide that help
- Ask — ask for help

The big prep question:

- "What do we want to learn from these guys?"

THANKS!

It's been fun. Thanks for reading :). I hope it was helpful. For slides, videos, and other information, check out momtestbook.com

When you hit a stumbling block I can help with or learn that I gave some bad advice, hit me up on twitter @robfitz or via email at rob@robfitz.com.

My blog where I write about early stage startup stuff is thestartuptoolkit.com. Subscribe to the rss or email updates and dig through the archive.

To learn to be a better founder, you've got to get your hands dirty. Startups are more craft than science. It's something you learn by doing. The tools help, but you need to get out in the field. I've learned more from launching silly projects than I ever did from reading books or blogs. Make it happen.

And finally, if you're in the business of supporting, training, mentoring, or investing in startups, I work with a few other founders building educational curriculum (slides, workshops, videos, facilitation guides, etc) at foundercentric.com. Download resources, join the mailing list, and get involved. We've run training from Costa Rica to Kiev with folks ranging from Oxford to the UN. Get in touch at hello@foundercentric.com.

ACKNOWLEDGMENTS

A huge thanks to all the people who helped with feedback, and especially those who took the time to write up their ridiculously useful line-by-line comments: Daniel Tenner, Andreas Klinger, Veronica Torras, Dave Chapman, Salim Virani, Sabrina Kiefer, Madeleine Evans, Spike Morelli, Adele Barlow, and Orsolya Toth. Thanks!

Nobody gets through the startup life alone. Thanks to Paul Graham for taking a punt on us when we were so clearly clueless and to Devin, Laurence, and Ryan for getting on that crazy train. Thanks to Saul Klein for lovingly yelling at me about sales every Friday and for forcing me to actually read *4 Steps to the Epiphany*. Thanks to Steve Blank for writing it. Thanks to Peter Read and Andy C for showing me how sales really works.

Thanks to Ian and Pete for getting us settled in London. Thanks to Salim Virani for calling me on my BS. Thanks to Tom Stone, Dave Chapman, John Spindler, and Tim Barnes for showing me the good bits of the startup education world and giving me my first chance to teach.

Beyond the obvious influence from Steve Blank and Eric

Ries, a big thanks to some other writers who have directly helped this book with their work: Amy Hoy on worldviews, Brant Cooper on segmentation, Richard Rumelt and Lafley/Martin on strategy, Neil Rackham on sales, and Derek Sivers on remembering that businesses are meant to make you happy.

And of course, big thanks for Mom & Dad for gently planting the entrepreneurial seed through both encouragement and their own collection of insane startup and/or shipwreck stories

The cover was put together by Devin Hunt. Author image by heisenbergmedia.com. Thanks!

Made in United States
Orlando, FL
16 February 2022